THE LAST NARC

THE LAST NARC

*A Memoir by the DEA's
Most Notorious Agent*

by Hector Berrellez

Published in collaboration with Renaissance Literary & Talent
Post Office Box 17379
Beverly Hills, CA 90209
www.renaissancemgmt.net

Copyright © 2020 by Hector Berrellez
Copyright Print on Demand Edition © 2020 by Hector Berrellez

ISBN: 978-1-950369-32-4

Cover art by Judy Bullard
www.customebookcovers.com

Edited by Jacklyn Saferstein-Hansen

All rights reserved. This book is sold subject to the condition that it shall not, by way of trade or otherwise, be lent, re-sold, hired out or otherwise circulated in any form of binding or cover other than that in which it is published and without a similar condition including this condition being imposed on the subsequent purchaser.

Contents

Praise	vii
Prologue & Acknowledgements	ix
Dedication	xiii
Part One: Birth	1
1. *La sombra,* The Shadow	3
2. *Antepasado,* Long Before	11
3. Made in Mexico	17
4. Wildcat	23
5. *La placa,* The Badge	33
6. *Las tres letras,* The Three Letters	47
7. *Desnudo en Tejas,* Naked in Texas	57
8. Ringside	69
9. The Day the DEA Stood Still	87
Part Two: Baptism	93
10. *Bienvenido a Mexico,* Welcome to Mexico	95
11. Cochi Loco and the Gipper	107
12. *Los tallos sangrientos,* The Bloody Stalks	125
13. Leyenda	143
Part Three: Confirmation	149
14. *Venganza,* Vengeance	151
15. *Los sospechosos,* The Suspects	155
16. *Nido de los alacránes,* The Scorpions' Nest	165
17. *Engañados,* Misled	175
18. *Sigue el dinero,* Follow the Money	193
19. *Secuestrar,* To Kidnap	197
20. *Veintitrés,* Twenty-three	203

Part Four: Death   209
21. *Arbusto ardiente*, Burning Bush   211
22. The Killing House   223
23. *Aguas*, Warning   231
24. Arrest of a Vicious Sicario   239
25. Betrayal   247
26. Death by Lead and Ink   257

Part Five: Resurrection   269
27. *Renacido*, Reborn   271
28. *Miedo a la verdad*, Fear of the Truth   279
29. *Vaquero*, Cowboy   285

Epilogue   289
Publisher's Note   299

Praise

"The truth about the 35-year-old murder of Kiki Camarena had to be told. Kiki deserves justice, deserves the truth. Hector made it his mission to expose what he discovered and how Kiki was and continues to be betrayed by those he trusted."

–Phil Jordan, former DEA agent

"Hector was an old-school, dedicated and fearless lawman. I'm glad he was on our side."

–Ed Heath, former supervisor, DEA, Mexico

"Hector Berrellez is a stone warrior, whose astonishing life story took him from the barrios of Tucson to the killing fields of Mexico and the halls of power in D.C. and into the heart of darkness of the most notorious murder in the history of the Drug War. He survived gunfights, assassination attempts and a deep state conspiracy. The fact that he lived to tell the tale is nothing short of miraculous."

–Tiller Russell, film director, *Operation Odessa, The Last Narc*

Prologue & Acknowledgements

My mother was a woman who could see the future. I am a man who is haunted by the past. It hasn't yet killed me, but it has debilitated me, seeping up and into my roots, poisoning me but keeping me alive. I thought of this last year when I watched Mexican drug kingpin Joaquín "El Chapo" Guzmán on TV as he was being extradited to the United States. He had been free for some time, having brazenly escaped from Altiplano, the maximum-security prison he was held at in Almoloya de Juárez, Mexico. Now he was being charged with over 17 drug-related charges on six separate indictments. But not one of those indictments or charges was his most egregious crime: conspiracy to commit the murder of federal agent Enrique Camarena, a fact I uncovered during my Operation Leyenda investigation.

El Chapo should not even be alive. He should be dead or rotting in jail somewhere. Instead, he smiles condescendingly as agents usher him from one international jurisdiction to the next. And why shouldn't he be? He's fat. Rosy-cheeked. Rich. And famous. In fact, he had just been featured in *Rolling Stone* magazine while on the lam, interviewed by Sean Penn. This is a man who boldly proclaimed, "I might not be the president of Mexico, but I am the boss." And as he's smiling while cameras follow him, in some twisted way, I think *he's smiling at me.*

The past will always haunt me.

All events seem to take on a life of their own. Events become stories. Stories become legend. And legend becomes myth. Cases too are like this. Operation Leyenda was not just a murder investigation. It was a microcosm of our country's misconceived War on Drugs, of our perception of good and evil, light and dark, heroes and villains. But lost somewhere in the translation and elevation of Leyenda was the truth.

People are not always comfortable with the truth. Americans in particular like our truth in black and white, right and wrong. When the veil of our preconceived notions of truth are lifted, it causes a paradigm shift in our world view. It challenges our faith. And it often leaves us morally confused and disconnected from the greater good that we all aspire to. I know this first hand.

History repeats itself. Until American drug policy changes, unfortunately, the events of Operation Leyenda will be played out in infinite loop. As the global narco-trade grows, the tragedies of these events will metastasize, no longer confined to Mexico and Central America.

They will be in Asia. Or Afghanistan. Or, in the case of the Obama administration's Hezbollah investigation, Project Cassandra, the Middle East. Some of these failures may come to light. Others, like Leyenda, may become legend. But it is important to remember that while the casualty of legend may be truth, the casualty behind truth is people: agents with families. Agents who are put in danger. Or compromised. Or even killed.

It has taken me almost 30 years to come to peace with the events of Leyenda. Though the wounds it left behind will never fully heal, I will no longer let it define me. I am proud of my service as a DEA agent. I am proud of what the agency stands for. And I am proud that I fought the good fight. Even so, if I could live my life all over again, I would turn down the assignment of Leyenda. That investigation cost me my career, destroyed my family and deeply penetrated my soul where my innocence was forever lost. I thank the Lord for one thing, and one thing only: that I was not extradited to Mexico by my government and murdered there to cover up what I discovered. My story would have died with me. Instead, within these pages, it lives.

My story would have also died had it not been for so many of the brave men and women of the DEA, who constantly risk their lives attempting to fulfill their dream of a drug free America for our citizens. Additionally, I want to individually thank Paul Gerard for helping me find my voice, Matt Ochacher for believing in me, and Tiller Russell and Eli Holtzman for bringing my story to life. My gratitude also goes to: Kenneth Starr, former United States Solicitor General, Bob Bonner, former Director of the U.S. Drug Enforcement Administration. And a special thanks to former Assistant United States Attorney Manny Medrano and his colleagues John Carlton, Jimmy Gurulé and Adam Schiff.

I would also like to mention Operation Leyenda Special Agents Doug Kuehl, Jim Spurr, Salvador Leyva, Marty Martinez, Wayne Schmidt, Tom Morales, Delbert Salazar, Susanna Baldwin, and all the other agents who helped the investigation. This also includes the good people of the Mexican Federal Judicial Police: Guillermo Gonzáles Calderoni, Florentino Ventura, Enrique Lopez and José Luis Larrazolo Rubio.

A heartfelt mention and thanks go to my closest DEA brothers: Phil Jordan, Ed Heath, Mike Holm, Mike Bansmer, and Eddie Follis and Art Berrellez. I trust you guys with my life and there is no one else I'd rather have on my side in a gun fight.

A special thanks to the team at Renaissance Literary and Talent: Alan Nevins, Jacklyn Saferstein-Hansen and Lauren Boone. You not only helped shape and polish this book, you facilitated getting it into the hands of the public so the truth could take flight.

Finally and most sincerely, I'd like thank my mother, Consuelo "Chatita" Berrellez. You will always be my North Star. To my sons Hector "Pinky" Berrellez, Christopher Berrellez, my lovely, wonderful daughter Crystal "Cuenita" Berrellez, and my grandson Hector "Little Hector" Berrellez. You guys are the reason I'm alive today.

–H. B.
April 2020

*For Gary Webb, Chuck Bowden and Hector Berrellez Sr.
Wish you guys were here.*

PART ONE

BIRTH

I am not yet born; O hear me.
Let not the man who is beast or who thinks he is God come near me.

–Louis MacNeice, "Prayer Before Birth"

Chapter 1

La sombra
The Shadow

The first time I killed a man was in the lush, mountainous terrain of Guadalajara in the state Jalisco, Mexico. It was early in my career, during my Arizona days. As an "undercover," you learn quickly and the hard way that no matter how carefully you plan an operation, you never know what's going to happen once it's underway. It's not Murphy's Law. *It's Murphy's Law on crystal meth.* You have to be prepared for everything — and even then shit can go sideways.

The DEA was running a joint operation with the Mexican military, which was common practice back then. My role was to buy of a lot of opium and a couple of tons of weed. The plan was that I'd go up a steep path to the top of a vine-covered mountain with my informant to meet the traffickers, make sure they had the drugs, then ask them to bring it down the road to a truck I had waiting at the bottom. Hidden in the jungle around the truck, I had about 20 Mexican *enterrados* armed with machine guns. When I gave the bust signal, they would swoop in and make the arrests.

Everything went according to plan at first. I went up the mountain with the informant, made sure the traffickers had the opium and weed, then told them to bring the drugs down the mountain to my truck where I assured them I had their money waiting. They bit.

So the informant and I went back down the road and we waited by my truck. And waited. After about 45 minutes, the traffickers finally came with the drugs, which were wrapped in white bed sheets and loaded on donkeys. When they reached the truck, I gave the bust signal as planned and my Mexican soldiers sprang from the jungle.

"*ALTO! POLICIA JUDICIA!*"

Which means, "STOP! JUDICIAL POLICE!"

But there was no "stop." All hell broke loose. In an instant, we were surrounded by machine gun fire. The traffickers had outsmarted us. Before we had even set up, they had stashed a dozen guys with AK-47s hidden around our perimeter in the jungle, just in case.

It was a big shootout, but it didn't last long. Maybe five minutes. During the battle, I shot and killed one of the *narcotraficante* gunmen, who was about 50 feet away. I shot him with my own AK-47.

Gunshots, unless to the head or heart, don't kill instantly. Many times guys don't even know they've been hit until a moment before they die. I saw this a lot during my time in the army. A soldier would get shot, but he would still continue fighting for a few moments before he suddenly collapsed. Once down, there would still be a few seconds before his life expired. Maybe it's the adrenaline. Or survival instincts. Or something else entirely. Maybe they need just a moment to process their life. Maybe it's that moment you hear people talking about, *their lives flashing before their eyes.* I don't know. All I know is that it's not a pleasant experience to see. And it is an even worse experience when *you cause it.*

There were dead men on both sides that day. The narcos lost more, but we lost some men too, though I don't remember exactly how many. I was raised Catholic, and the emotional aftermath of killing that man in the jungle — my first kill — hit me hard. But not at that moment. In the aftermath of a battle, there is no space for regret, or penance, or deep moral musing. It is the opposite. Guys pat each other on the back and play to your ego. "Way to go man, you got your first one!" And all that other macho shit. "Did you see I blew that motherfucker away?" And by the time you get back to the safe confines of your office or your home, you've tucked the whole thing away.

After a few years working the border, there were more shootouts, and more killing. Each one got a little bit easier. I would just keep telling myself, *it was a part of the job.* But this all changed the day I shot and killed a drug trafficker, whose name I didn't even know.

· · · · ·

There was a case in Riverside, California where two undercover agents had been trying to bust a ring of Sinaloan cowboys supplying heroin to the San Bernardino Valley. The two agents were Billy Terrazas, who was Mexican and spoke Spanish, and his partner Bobby Bags, who was white and only spoke English. After months trying to penetrate the ring, the pair finally managed to buy a sample of heroin from the cowboys under the agreement that if it came back pure, they would commit to buying three kilos.

The lab results came back at 90% pure and a deal was set. But before they could make the arrangements for the buy/bust, Billy Terrazas was called away to work a higher priority case. Bobby Bags and the Riverside agents still wanted to bust the Sinaloans, but to do so they needed a Hispanic, Spanish-speaking agent. So the DEA sent me.

I had worked with Bobby before and I liked him. Though he was a relatively unseasoned undercover agent with only four years of experience, there was no doubt in my mind that he loved his job. As an undercover, or "UC," he dressed in loud, expensive clothes, slicked his hair back and wore a gold rope around his neck as thick as a garden hose. By then, my undercover character had evolved a bit too. "Manny" was now a ball-breaking Mexican dealer who got shit done.

The DEA in Riverside brought me up to speed quickly, detailing the entire operation and the traffickers involved. Typically, it's never a good move to bring in a new player to either side of an equation in a drug deal. Both buyers and sellers are highly paranoid — and rightly so. But Bobby felt in his gut that the Sinaloans would still deal. There was money on the line now and you didn't have to be an undercover long to understand that *no trafficker ever said no to money.*

The Sinaloan cowboys operated out of a shoddy apartment in one of those places that we should have taken a flame-thrower to. It was a small, two-story cesspool located in Fontana. The black Mercedes Benz we pulled into the parking lot with was probably worth more than the entire apartment complex.

The plan was set: We'd send the informant up to the apartment where the Sinaloans were holed up to make sure they had the kilos of heroin. If they did, he would tell them we had the cash in the trunk of the car outside. The bust team was already set up and in their positions, about 15 agents, armed and ready. The signal would be Bobby opening up the trunk.

· · · · ·

The delay is always the hardest part of a bust. Neither Bobby nor I would ever say it out loud, but as we waited in the car for dealers to come down, we both thought the same thing: *What if they know? What if they're on to us?* This anxiety only grows with every extra minute of waiting. Bobby and I sat in the parking lot outside that apartment complex for almost 20 minutes that day. Had it been any longer, we might have pulled the plug. But just then, the informant appeared from the apartment — *without the Sinaloans*. I rolled down my window and he leaned in.

"They got the heroin, but they don't want to come down. They want you to *come up* — and bring the money with you."

I looked at Bobby and he shrugged. It was my call. I stepped out of the car.

The informant walked me to the Sinaloans' apartment upstairs. As soon as we entered, three sets of badass-looking Mexican eyes glared my way. Each one was covered in jackhouse ink and was either holding a gun or had one in front of him. They had never seen me before, so naturally, one of them said in Spanish, "Who the fuck are you?"

"I told you guys, Pablo is sick," the informant said. "He's in the hospital, so Manny here came instead."

They looked me over some more until another one said, "So who the fuck is Manny then?"

"Manny is the one who has the money," I said. "That's who Manny is. So if you want to do this shit, let's do it."

"Okay, where's the money, Manny?" he asked.

"It's in the trunk of my car."

"Go get it. Because we ain't givin' you shit until we get paid."

I saw where this was going and ended it. "Listen to me. I ain't playing that game. I'm going back to my car. If you don't bring the heroin outside in the next five minutes, the deal is off."

I turned to the informant and added loud enough for them to hear, "See if you can talk some sense into these motherfuckers."

· · · · ·

Less than five minutes later, I was sitting in the car with Bobby when the informant came out of the apartment again — this time with the Sinaloans, one of whom was carrying a small backpack. We stepped out of our car and moved to the trunk.

The Sinaloans approached and the one carrying the backpack said, "Okay, Manny. Here's your heroin."

That's when I messed up. I reached out and took the backpack. To this day, I regret that I did, because it was a tactical mistake: It occupied my hands. But I looked in the bag, saw the heroin and nodded the okay to Bobby. He turned, put the key in the trunk, popped it. And within a second, the bust team rushed at us from all directions, aiming shotguns and rifles and yelling, "DEA!"

The cowboy who'd handed me the backpack yelled in Spanish, *"Manny, son los perros!"* which means "here come the dogs," but is also slang for *here come the police.* As soon as he yelled it, he pulled out his gun right in front of me and took aim.

Because I was holding the backpack with the heroin in my right hand, which is my dominant hand, I couldn't reach for my gun. Instead, I pushed his arm with my left hand to disrupt his shot. It went wild. I dropped the backpack, pulled my .357 Magnum and shot him twice in the stomach. He staggered back. Bobby fired another quick burst and I unloaded my clip. As I did, I saw parts of the cowboy's body exploding off of him. He went down.

The other two Sinaloans tried to run but Bobby chased after them. They didn't even get as far as the end of the parking lot before the bust team was all over them. While they cuffed and gathered them, I walked up to the man we'd shot and discovered he was still alive. He still had the gun in his hand, so I stepped on his arm and bent down. He looked up at me and said, "I'm sorry, Manny." His eyes rolled back and he died.

This is a moment I relive over and over again. *Why did he say that? Did he not know that I had shot him? Did he think I was a criminal like him and might be going to jail now? Or did he realize I was a cop and he was apologizing for being a criminal?* It could have been any of these things, or none of them. Maybe all that mattered was that my face was the last one he was going to see in this life and he just wanted to apologize for something, or to someone, before he died, like a last confession.

I was deeply affected by the death of that Sinaloan cowboy. For months after we had shot him, I would stop and think to myself, *what have I done?* According to the law of man, I had every right to kill that cowboy. He was a drug trafficker. A criminal. And he most likely would have shot and killed me if I had not ended his life. *But what about God's law? What did He think of what I'd done?* Maybe, had I not taken that bag of heroin like I did, my hands would have been free. I could have pulled my gun out at the bust signal, beating him to the draw, and he would have never reached for his piece. I didn't mention any of this later in the day when I wrote out my investigation report, known as a DEA-6. I just stuck to the facts, referring to him only as "the armed suspect."

I tell this story first because regret is a strange emotion. While it is never overwhelming, it's something that I've discovered is far more powerful. *It is unrelenting.* You don't carry regret like grief or pain. You can't put it down. It follows you like a shadow. *La sombra.* I tried to ignore that shadow for most of my professional life as a lawman. At times I've even tried to drink it away. Or pray it away. Or kill it away. I even thought that by talking about my shadow, by telling my story and bringing it out of the darkness, that it might disappear. Unfortunately, all the light in the world can never make some shadows go away. So I did something different: *I embraced it.* In a standard psychological review after the incident, I was asked by the examiner as to why I had shot the cowboy ten times. I answered, half-jokingly, "Because I ran out of bullets."

Only now that I am an older man can I see how much pain and suffering all the violence had caused me. And all of it makes me want to go back to the beginning.

Back when I was light and there was no shadow.

Chapter 2

Antepasado
Long Before

Matan a su padre.
Matan a sus hermanos.
Roban a su ganado.
Violan a sus mujeres.

They kill your father.
They kill your brothers.
They steal your cattle.
They rape your women.

–Lyrics from a Mexican folk song

I was not the first Berrellez to be betrayed by his country. That wound was formed inside me long before I was born. His name was Nicolas Antonio Berreyesa and he was the first of my ancestors to be born in North America. Sinaloa, Mexico to be exact. The year was 1761.

Antonio was a born cowboy, a *vaquero,* a fearless man who rode herd on the wild longhorn cattle that once roamed the foothills of the Sierra Madre Occidental. But he had adventure in his heart and moved up to Spanish California as part of the renowned De Anza Colonization Expedition. He wasn't even 16 yet.

At this time, the American colonies were at war with England. It would quickly spread into a worldwide conflict. France sided with the colonies. And in turn, Spain too would declare war on England. King Carlos III of Spain wanted to reinforce the California settlements of "New Spain" and established a presidio at Santa Barbara. My eight-times great grandfather Antonio was one of the 250 soldiers who served there. As a direct descendant of his, I am entitled to join the South Coast Chapter of the Sons of the Revolution.

After the war, Antonio married, moved north and settled with other *rancheros* in the arcadian landscape of *Cañada de Capay,* "The Valley of the Stream," the Napa Valley today. For a brief period, my ancestors lived the dream of all people. They farmed rich land. They lived in peace. They thrived. Their eldest son, Reyes Berreyesa, won the heart of one Maria Zacarias Bernal, whose family had also been prosperous. The couple had 13 children. Within one generation, the Berreyesa family was one of the wealthiest and most influential in all of Spanish California.

But their dream was not meant to last.

Los Osos, as Spanish Californians called them, the "bear flaggers," had always been coming West — even long before the gold rush. Like my ancestors before them, these settlers were largely immigrants and adventurers, and as a whole, they were some of America's finest goodwill ambassadors. They were hardy men who worked the land given them and were readily accepted. Many were on their best behavior as they tried to court the beautiful, dark-eyed daughters of the New Spaniards. To be accepted by a Mexican woman's father was a great badge of honor. But in 1846, a new wave of migration was coming from the East. This group of *"Americanos"* was not like the eager settlers that had come before them. They came with bad intentions. And they came on the dime of the U.S. government.

Captain John C. Frémont led the four expeditions into the American West. Frémont was a widely admired explorer, politician and soldier. His expedition into Spanish California was said to be for geological research. But Frémont brought no such experts with him. He brought outlaws and gunmen. *Frémont wanted land.* And he was sanctioned to do whatever he could to acquire it.

On June 14th, 1846, three of Reyes and Maria's sons were ambushed in Sonoma by *Los Osos*, taken to San Rafael and imprisoned. The surprise attack wasn't random. At the time of this unlawful act, the Berreyesa family owned and operated the three largest cattle ranches in the West. Reyes was 75 years old, but he gathered his gun, mounted his horse and went after his boys. Two of his nephews, Francisco and Ramon de Haro, would join him.

Upon reaching Sonoma, Reyes decided to leave his guns before he proceeded on. He did not want to provoke Frémont's men and firmly believed that the *Americanos* had no reason to shoot them — especially if they showed up in peace. So the trio continued toward San Rafael unarmed.

Along the way, they were spotted by *Los Osos*, whose man in charge was the well-known frontiersman Kit Carson. Carson and his men had been sent to San Rafael as Frémont's reinforcements and were instructed to intercept any Californians that might obstruct his "interests." Before Carson went on his way, he asked Frémont, "Captain, shall I take prisoners?"

Frémont replied with a wave of his hand. "We have no room for prisoners." Carson did not like the order. But he would follow it.

Reyes knew he was in trouble the moment he saw Carson and his men approach them. As a former sergeant in the army, he quickly recognized that these *Americanos* were neither soldiers nor explorers. These bear flaggers were rag-torn mountain men *and they were there to kill him.* He knew right then that he had made a mistake leaving his guns behind. With as much dignity as he could muster, he appealed to Kit Carson. He asked him to take his life and spare those of his nephews. Carson did not honor the request. Instead, he and his group shot one of the first generation sons of the American Revolution, Reyes Berreyesa, and his two nephews in cold blood.

• • • • •

I did not know the story of my ancestors for much of my life. Consequently, I grew up with a very idyllic sense of good and evil, right and wrong. This philosophy was only reinforced by my Roman Catholic upbringing, which laid the fertile ground from which I would grow into a lawman. Little did I know the past would not only contribute to my present, but also to my future. In time I would discover that though my ancestors' story was apart from me, *it was also a part of me.* That original sin of betrayal has been etched somewhere along the double helix of my DNA. But so too has their sense of adventure. Their heroism. Their love of family. Their faith in God. By proxy, in some strange way that I do not understand, I too am a part of their story. I am not the realization of their dream, but rather a continuation of it.

It has taken me a lifetime to understand how the past and present are chained together. For me, the story of my Berreyesa ancestors is the most important link in this chain. It is a chain that includes the magic of adventure, the sum of sacrifice, the pain of loss and betrayal, and the poetry of faith. And it was all forged long before I existed.

Chapter 3

Made in Mexico

My family and I may have been the first Mexicans to have actually been deported *from Mexico to the United States*. My mother, Consuelo, was born in Phoenix, Arizona to parents Goytia and Eufemio Gonzales, who were illegal immigrants. When she was four years old, U.S. Border Patrol picked the family up and deported them to Mexico — even though, legally, she and her two sisters were American citizens. They ended up in Nogales, Sonora and settled there.

My grandparents were fiercely Roman Catholic, instilling in my mother a deeply held reverence for holy days of obligation, Lent and Our Lady of Guadalupe. My grandmother was particularly fervent, especially after the sudden death of my grandfather. She raised her girls on a strict diet of prayer, cooking, weaving and preparing for motherhood. Under my grandmother's watch there would be no possibility of any of the Gonzales girls becoming pregnant without marriage before their *quinceañera*.

My mom almost made it.

Around that time she had met a local boy named Hector Berrellez. He was a quiet, well-read brooder who worked hard and loved boxing. Though he didn't talk much, he possessed the restrained charisma of an *encantador,* a real Mexican charmer. Her

Catholicism notwithstanding, my mom soon found herself pregnant. When my grandmother found out, she did what any good Mexican mother would do: She kicked the girl out of the house. My parents were taken in by gypsies for a time until they were discovered again — this time by Mexican Border Patrol. They ran a routine check on my mom and found out that she was born in Arizona.

"You're not Mexican," they told her. "You're American."

This was news to her.

They sent the three of us to the United States. My father. My mother. And me, though I hadn't been born yet.

· · · · ·

I grew up in the barrio of South Tucson, Arizona where my father found work as a bricklayer. My mother, having learned from the gypsies she stayed with briefly, told fortunes — a gift it was said she was extremely proficient in. Once our family had settled, five more boys followed. We were not rich by any means, but we were long from wanting. South Tucson in the 1960s was a good place for a boy to live. The racial tensions that were fomenting all across the country from Watts to Detroit had not yet permeated our city. Or maybe they had and just evaporated under the Old Pueblo sun. South Tucson had always been a melting pot. On any given day, up to five different flags could be seen waving atop buildings: American, Mexican, Spanish, Confederate and the State of Arizona.

As a boy, my first run-in with the law was a memorable one. My brothers and I were out and about one day in the summer, doing what bored boys do, looking for something stupid to get into.

Somewhere in our travels we had come across an odd assemblage of items that included rolls of toilet paper, matches and alcohol. One need not have my mother's gift to imagine what happened next.

My brothers and I managed to outrun the firemen, but not the South Tucson P.D. In a routine number department cops often pulled with budding juvenile delinquents, we were dragged into the station, yelled at and even slapped around a bit. It was meant to scare us. And scared we were — *to go home.* We begged the police to let us walk home. If our old man saw any of his boys being dropped off in a police car, there would be hell to pay.

The cops not only refused, they filed all of us into one of their squad cars. The driver even popped on the misery lights. We went home to an ass-whupping and a half — but none more so than me, who as the oldest bore the most responsibility. The sting of that beating stayed with me for a long time. If you would have asked me then what I wanted to do with my life when I got older, the last answer you would have ever received was *police officer.*

• • • • •

Though I didn't know it, I was born with the requisite seeds of being an undercover. As I would find out later in life, being a UC was a gift no different than being musical or athletic. You either had it or you didn't. But it was my father who definitely watered the seeds in my latent skill set. It began when I was in grade school, and as so many of boyhood's life-lessons are learned, this too came as a result of being bullied.

For months it seemed, maybe years, I had been chronically harassed and beaten up after school by an older, bigger boy. So often had it happened that it simply became a part of my routine. Hell, there was even a rhythm to it. *Bell ring. Exit school. Eat shit. Take punch. Go home.* But the routine ended abruptly one day when my father happened to be home. At seeing his disheveled eldest son still bleeding from the nose, he asked me, *"What the hell happened?"* I told my dad everything: about how the bully followed me out of school, teased me for a bit, then beat on me in the exact same spot every day. With his temperature and blood pressure rising, he stared at me.

"Get in the truck and take me there," he said.

I swallowed what little there was of my pride, got in our family truck and took my father to the site of my suffering.

Once we got there, my father looked around. *"This the spot?"*

I nodded sheepishly. It was a small patch of dirt just outside the school's boundaries. My father went to the back of his truck, grabbed what could have been a shovel and violently broke off the wooden handle.

He walked over to me and said, *"You see this stick? We're going to hide it in that mesquite tree right there."*

I hadn't even noticed, but there was some desert brush nearby.

"Tomorrow when that boy follows you out here, you go to that tree, grab this stick and you beat his ass with it. Do you understand me?" Only he didn't phrase it like a question.

Now, I was not a fighter. I was afraid of the bigger, older boy. But I was scared shitless of my father. If I managed to get my ass whipped again by the bully, I would probably face an even bigger beating from my old man. So there was no doubt what I was going to do.

Like clockwork, after the school bell rang at the end of the next day, the bully appeared. Per the ordinary course of action, he badgered me, then followed me to the place of my punishment. But on this day, when he brought me to the spot, I wandered off course a tad, proceeding to the base of the mesquite tree. I reached in. Like an unsuspecting fish, the bully followed. *"What the hell are you doing?"* he asked. And like Excalibur, I pulled out the shovel handle, or whatever the hell it was, glared at my tormentor and swung as hard as I could.

I may have floated home. I don't remember. All I do remember is that when I got there my father was waiting for me. But he didn't look pleased. We studied one another.

"*So you beat his ass?*" he asked.

I nodded and my father's face bent into a slight smile.

"*That's good. But real men don't fight with sticks. Come here.*"

I moved close to my father, who bent down and whispered to me as if he were sharing the secrets to a buried treasure.

"*I'm going to teach you how to box now. But you are never going to tell anyone. Ever. Do you understand?*"

I nodded.

"*Now put your hands up.*"

My father showed me how to square up a la Marquis de Queensbury.

"*Your first lesson is the jab,*" he said. "*Straight out, from the shoulder. GO.*"

So I began to jab.

I would learn how to box quite well, but I would never tell anyone. And though I loved being able to defend myself, the power of keeping my skills a secret was just as exhilarating. The ability to keep a secret was something I would nurture. It was a skill I would need in the future. I didn't know it at the time, but my life would depend on it.

And I would always keep a stick hidden in the bushes.

Chapter 4

Wildcat

I graduated from Pueblo High School in 1966. Unlike a lot of my classmates and even many from my generation, *I knew exactly what I wanted to do.* I wanted to make money. So I enrolled at the University of Arizona in the fall of that year with the intent to study business administration. The Vietnam War had just begun to heat up and President Johnson was amping up the draft. I wasn't too worried yet. The "anti-war" movement wasn't near the fever pitch it would reach. Hell, most of us thought it would just blow over. Still, I applied for and was granted a 2-S deferment so I could start my education.

My first year of college was one of the best experiences of my life. I was just a kid from the barrio in South Tucson and it was so exciting to be around people from all different walks of life and from all over the state. There was a vibrant, collective energy that we all seemed to share. It was the common belief that *we could do anything.* Everyone was away from their families and their homes and all thrown onto this beautiful campus. I really loved it. You would think that a college campus in the late '60s would be full of protests and drugs and free love. *I wish.* In retrospect, it was one of the most innocent times of my life.

The highlight of my first year at Arizona was forming a rock and roll band. As I entered my teens, I became obsessed with music. I had grown up listening to Little Richard and Buddy Holly and Jackie Wilson. But it would be the Beatles that made me want to buy a guitar and learn how to play. To pay for one, I borrowed a couple of bucks from my old man, bought some Kiwi shoe polish, grabbed an old shoe box and went to work. I would go the local watering holes after school, put my box down and charge .25 cents for a shine. *And what kind of guy would turn down a hard working neighborhood kid for a cheap shine?* Turns out not too many. I had never shined a shoe before in my life. Working with that Kiwi polish was like working with a paintbrush. You had to squeeze the polish out of the bottle and apply it through its spongey tip. It always came out uneven and I always ended up getting the shit all over the men's socks. Fortunately for me, by the time word spread that I was the lousiest shoe shiner in all of South Tucson, I had already made enough to buy my first guitar. I taught myself a few chords and actually got pretty decent. Or at least I thought.

The big hangout for musicians on campus was at a place called the Dungeon. And that's where I met who would become my best friend, Arturo Meyer. Art was one of the best live performers I had ever seen. He was good looking, could sing and man could he dance. He was like a Mexican James Brown. We met after one of his gigs one night and became thick as thieves. We picked up a drummer and a bass player and started a band called the Beathovens. We thought it was clever because we mostly did Beatles covers. There was another kid I had known from back home named Manny Quesney who wanted to join too. Manny was one of those guys who was just always around — no matter what we were

The Last Narc

doing, he wanted to be included. He was a good dude, but never quite fit in. We also thought he didn't have the chops to be in our band, but since we liked him, we made him our roadie. Though I was taking my education seriously, music and the band were really becoming my passion. With Art as our lead singer, I thought we may have had a shot. We were getting small gigs all over Tucson, playing at dive bars and frat parties. And we had become a crowd favorite at the Dungeon. A lot of people and other bands were taking notice. One of them was one of the most beautiful women I had ever seen in my life. Her name was Linda Córdova. She was a 5-10 stunner, big blue eyes, body from hell. She was a singer in one of our rival bands called the Relatives. Their band wasn't very good but everyone loved its lead singer, including my best friend Art, who had always carried a torch for her. One night in between sets, Linda approached and asked if she could sing with us. I don't think she finished the question before we pushed her on stage and handed her a microphone. We asked what she wanted to sing and she said, "La Bamba." As Mexicans, that was a song we all grew up with and could really rock out. Well, we did. And we floored the place. Everyone went crazy. By the time we finished, I was plotting to rob a bank so I could buy this girl Linda a ring. Afterwards, I pulled her aside.

"Linda, you were great." She thanked me. "How about you join our band?"

She was flattered but passed. I made my play.

"Well, how about we go out?" Again she was flattered. But she knew Art also liked her and she knew Art and I were best friends.

"What about Art?" she asked.

Art. Art who?

Alas, she passed again. I never saw her again after that. But I kept tabs on that gal Linda Córdova. A couple of years later she would change her last name to Carter. She would go on to win the Miss USA pageant, move to Hollywood and become Wonder Woman. That was all well and good. But man, you should have heard her sing "La Bamba."

There was one other gal named Linda who also came into our orbit while at Arizona. She was a chubby little white chick with dimples who sang as part of a local family act called the New Union Ramblers. The Dungeon had held a "battle of the bands" contest and we thought the Beathovens were a shoo-in to win. We didn't. We lost to the chubby, dimpled girl and her siblings. Yeah, she could sing, I thought. *But she'll never make it.*

Her name was Linda Ronstadt.

• • • • •

That first year at U of A flew by. And with my 2-SD expired, I was drafted. By this time, I had grown concerned about the war. Vietnam was becoming a hot-button issue in our country. Everyone knew a lot of young men were going over and a lot them weren't coming back. But I thought it was my civic responsibility to serve my country. I loved being American and though I didn't know anything about politics or the war, I knew *I had to go.* My best friend Art did not have to go. Toward the end of our first year he had met a girl, fallen in love and gotten married. He could have automatically been eligible for deferment. But Art didn't apply for one. He said to me, *"Hector, if you're going to war, I'm going to war."* He volunteered to serve in the Army. It was one of the most touching things anyone had ever done for me. To honor him, I listed Art as my "escort" in the event something happened to me while in service.

As part of the draft process, I took a battery of tests and scored high enough to be placed in Officer Candidate School (OCS). I was then sent to San Antonio, Texas where I trained to be a combat field medic. This was both a blessing and a curse. Coming out of OCS would look impressive on my resume. But being a combat field medic in a dangerous hot zone like Vietnam meant I might never get to use it. As deployment neared, fear crept in. It came to a crescendo about three days before I left when my unit, the 76th Artillery, was told rather abruptly that *we were not going to Vietnam. We were going somewhere more dangerous.*

In January of 1968, North Korean forces seized an American navy vessel and captured its 83 crew members in what is known today as the "Pueblo Incident." I was going to be part of a force that would be deployed north of the 38th parallel. While this area was supposed to be a demilitarized zone, it was one of the most volatile and life-threatening in all of central Asia, a communist badland. Suddenly, Vietnam didn't sound so bad anymore.

As it would turn out, North Korea would blink in the face of American might. And though tensions were escalated, the engagement would end without incident. But I stayed above the 38th with my unit as part of a small American military presence and experienced my share of war and all its hideous offerings. Firefights were a regular affair. Sometimes between us and the Vietcong who attacked from the South. Sometimes with the Koreans in the North. And sometimes between North Koreans and South Koreans. I tended to men with their legs blown off. Men with their torsos ripped open by shrapnel. Even men who had been impaled by punji stakes in what were "death traps." In my short time spent in service, I would see more death and carnage than I would ever care to see.

Then one day it stopped.

Not even nine months into my tour, I was called into the chaplain's tent. I knew immediately what this meant. *Someone in my family had died.* I was sure it was my father, who had always lived a tough life. As I walked toward the tent, I prepared myself for this news. But when I got there, I found out it was someone else. *Art Meyer had been killed in battle.* As I had done for Art, he too listed my name as his military escort in the event of his death. I now had to take Art back to his family.

As I moved into manhood, my world was growing but it never overwhelmed me. It had always been my family, and then school, and then college. Even as I was far from home and in the middle of serving in a war, the world still never seemed that big. That was until the day I had to positively identify my best friend Art Meyer's body. Under military escort, I was flown to the U.S. port in Okinawa's capital, Naha. I didn't know this, but Naha had been the central nerve center for the Vietnam War and it was the most active base I had ever seen. As I was led toward the hangar where the deceased soldiers were, I noticed a large area that was nicknamed "The Bone Yard." It was like a gigantic junkyard for military vehicles. There were mountains of crushed jeeps and burnt out trucks — many covered in blood and bullet holes.

Stepping into the hangar where Art's body was waiting to be identified changed my life. As soon as I walked in I saw what must have been hundreds of wooden coffins, all neatly stacked up and placed in rows like a library. I stood there for a long moment and only then did I realize how many families would be forever changed by what was happening, and how far-reaching the pain was. I stood there, stunned, when an MP appeared in front of me.

"Who are you here for?" he asked.

I told him PFC Art Meyer.

"This is just A to L," he said. "The Ms are next door."

· · · · ·

I arrived in Tacoma, Washington two days later as the official military escort of Private First Class Arturo Meyer. I had been flown via U.S. transport plane but in a weird twist I hadn't expected, once I landed in Tacoma, I had to fly the last leg to Arizona commercial. That meant Art's body had to be checked in as regular luggage. Seriously. After the plane landed in Tucson, I had to go to baggage claim with the rest of the civilian passengers. It was beyond bizarre, all of us waiting for our luggage, huddled over the conveyor.

Suitcase… Golf clubs… Baby carriage… Dead body.

Most of Art's family had shown up at the airport to retrieve their loved one. Their grieving had already started, but many of them were not fully prepared for the moment they would see the body. It was heartbreaking. Art's parents were there as were several of his siblings and some other folks who might have been relatives or friends, including our friend and bandmate Manny Quesney's parents. Most wept quietly and some said prayers. Others stood there silently, offering only their presence. I did neither. I could only watch. Art's mother was particularly moving in her grief. I knew right then that this wound would never heal for her. I wanted to reach out and embrace her. As I would find out in due time, some arms cannot reach around that kind of pain.

Before they parted, Art's father shook my hand and thanked me. Several other members of his family also expressed their gratitude. Just then, it occurred to me that Art's wife Marie wasn't there. I had only met Marie briefly after Art had fallen in love with her. She was a beautiful, kind woman who made Art very happy. So I asked Mr. Meyer where she was.

"She's in the hospital," he told me.

My first thought was that the horrible news of her husband had overtaken her. But it was worse. "She's giving birth to their first child."

He thanked me again and I watched as they all walked away. Manny's parents stayed behind for a moment before approaching me solemnly. They asked me how I was holding up, how the war effort was going. I tried to posture the strong soldier, but at 20, I was still just a kid. I thanked them for showing support for Art's family, but they told me that was only one of the reasons they were there. *They had come to see me.* Why, I wondered. My childhood friend and bandmate Manny had been killed while escorting Art's body from Japan. Like Art, he too had put my name down as his escort in the event of his death. *He wanted so badly to be like one of us.* Even in the end.

Only on the flight back to Japan did it all hit me. Staring at the world beneath, I thought about my place in it all. Just a year earlier I was having the time of my life, studying in college, playing in a rock and roll band, my future brimming with hope. Now here I was, alone. Uncertain. Frightened. And as I sat there thinking, I did what was very unbecoming of a man. A soldier. A combat medic. I wept.

Chapter 5

La placa
The Badge

I was honorably discharged from the U.S. Army in August of 1969, and not that I had anywhere else to go, I headed home to South Tucson because my father had broken his back. He had been on a scaffold while working a job and fell off. He was the prime bread winner in our family, so every able-bodied Berrellez needed to chip in.

I immediately started looking into jobs. My first choice, and pretty much the first choice of every kid coming out of the barrio, was in the mines. It was hard, dirty work. One of my brothers had gotten a job there while I was away and he didn't even last a day. But it paid well and they were always looking for workers. I knew I could get the job and I almost drove straight over when an ad in the classifieds caught my attention. The South Tucson Police were hiring.

I went to the same station where my brothers and I had all been taken back when we set those toilet paper rolls on fire. In fact, I was interviewed in the same room where the policemen had shaken us down. That memory put a smile on my face as I listened to the supervising police officer talk about the joys and responsibilities of being a cop.

As fate would have it, the South Tucson Police Department loved me. They loved that I was bilingual. They loved that I had served in the military. And they loved that I would be willing to work any shift so long as I had time to continue my education. For me too, it was a match made in heaven. South Tucson wasn't exactly New York City. I would probably end up giving tickets and arresting most of the guys I grew up with. But the job allowed me to stay at home, help my family and continue my education. I still had no intention of making police work a career. I had other plans. *Bigger plans.*

· · · · ·

I went through the academy with no problem and became a small town police officer. Though I didn't think I would like it much, I was wrong. *I loved it.* There was something about putting on that uniform. Wearing that badge, *I was one of the good guys.* Now everybody knew it. My mother was beside herself. *"Oh, Memin! Estoy muy orgullosa!"* Yes, she was proud. But what really made her happy was that I was still at home.

I didn't know what to expect being a cop in my hometown. I figured I would just be arresting some of the same people I'd grown up with. And that was pretty much the case. One of my first big "collars" was an armed robbery suspect I had known since childhood. His name was Mark Ortiz and he had been dating a local gal who worked at the Salvation Army. When she dumped him, he got pissed and wanted to do something about it. So he got a gun, put on a ski mask and robbed the Salvation Army when she was working. It was a big deal. South Tucson may have been on the poorer side, but people didn't run around with guns and rob stores. The whole department dropped what they were doing and went on a massive manhunt. It was even "breaking news" on the local channels. I was off the clock, in my room studying when I heard my mom yell, "*Memin, phone call!*"

"Who is it, ma?" I asked.

"It's Mrs. Ortiz. She wants to talk to you!"

Mrs. Ortiz informed me that Mark had made a mistake and would like to turn himself in — but only to me. I said okay and asked where he was. She told me he was hiding under his bed. So I went over there, picked him up and drove him to the precinct. I didn't even bother to throw on my uniform. I just walked him in with my jeans, tee shirt and gun. I didn't think anything of it, but everyone was looking at me like I was fucking Serpico or something.

I worked the force for a couple of years and even made homicide detective, becoming the youngest in the history of the department. After solving a few cases, I decided I wanted to join a bigger department, so I got a job with the Arizona Department of Safety as a state highway patrol officer. It wasn't as exciting as being a cop. I did routine detail, investigating highway accidents, writing speeding tickets, that kind of stuff, but it was also a hike in pay and prestige, both of which were helpful to my family and career. I still didn't want a career in law enforcement, but I had taken an interest in law. My plan was to finish up my degree and apply to law school after I graduated. My life changed course when the Arizona State Police drug unit in Tucson contacted my superiors. They didn't have any undercover officers who could speak Spanish. Go figure. My superiors recommended me.

⋅ ⋅ ⋅ ⋅ ⋅

When my sergeant asked me if I was sure about going undercover, I said no problem. I didn't consider that I had never trained in undercover tactics. I was 25 at the time, young and macho and stupid — you know, all the things that make you think you're really cool when you're younger. Another reason I accepted the assignment was that illegal drugs had deeply affected my own family. While I had been away in the army, unbeknown to me, my youngest brother was introduced to heroin by a Cuban drug dealer in the barrio. He was only 13. His subsequent addiction resulted in years spent in and out of prison and much pain for my mother and father. After I became a South Tucson police officer, even though I wasn't narc or vice, I spent time trying to track down that Cuban dealer but found out he had fled the country. The situation was something that had haunted me since I returned from the service and I wanted to do something about it. I had literally zero preparation for going undercover in the state's drug program. On the first day of my first assignment, when I showed up for work, they said, "Take off your uniform, you're working drug unit this week."

I started doing small-time undercover buys. I'd work a week here and there, make some buys for the team, then they'd send me back to uniformed duty. It was crazy. I'd buy an ounce of marijuana or heroin or cocaine one week and then be back in my highway patrol car the next week, giving out speeding tickets. I'm lucky I was never recognized and killed.

After almost two years doing this kind of undercover work, the Tucson unit finally hooked a bigger fish. They had flipped an informant who offered up information on a drug trafficker, a

Mexican lawyer who'd been importing heroin into the U.S. for several years. The informant offered to introduce an undercover policeman to this lawyer, but he was very clear that the undercover needed to be Hispanic and speak Spanish, because there was no way this lawyer from Sinaloa was going to trust a white guy.

According to the informant, the lawyer was from Sinaloa and a serious dealer. He was moving kilos across state lines, which made it a federal case. The Department of Public Safety brought me in to do the buy and due to the amount of drugs involved, they alerted the Bureau of Narcotics and Dangerous Drugs (BNDD). The BNDD agent assigned to the case was named John Zinter. but the Tucson unit made it very clear that the bust was *theirs*.

The informant spoke with the Mexican dealer and mentioned that he had found another buyer who could potentially move a lot of weight. The dealer was interested but wanted to "test the waters" first and offered to sell an ounce of pure heroin for $10,000. If the deal went well, only then would he commit to a bigger deal. That was fine for the Tucson unit. They planned a very simple buy/bust, with the BNDD fronting me $10,000 for the purchase. Once the dope and money were exchanged, I would light a cigarette to signal the bust.

Though I had some experience buying dope, I knew I couldn't pass myself off as a seasoned drug dealer, so I created an alter-ego named Manny, a Mexican-American kid from South Tucson who had friends in the Italian mafia in Chicago. Manny was dumb, inexperienced and afraid. The polar opposite of me, who thought he was smart, savvy and fearless. Manny was also doing the drug deal to make money for his sick mother. Cue violins.

• • • • •

I, Manny, was introduced by the informant to the Mexican drug dealer in a public parking lot in downtown Tucson. He was around 50 years old and looked the part of a professional attorney, sharply dressed, well spoken. I, on the other hand, looked nothing like a drug dealer — something he picked up on right away. "You don't seem very comfortable, Manny," he said. "What are you doing mixed up in this shit?"

I offered my prepared story. "I'm only involved in this because my mom is sick. She has cancer and we have no insurance. I'm just trying to make some money to cover her doctor bills. I don't even smoke marijuana." I told him about my Italian friends, how the deal was just a "one and done" for me and that I didn't want to be in the dope game.

"Okay, okay, don't worry about it," he said, then showed me his ounce of heroin. "You see this? It's 90% pure. Your Italian guys are going to love it, I promise you. If they do, you tell them we can do all the kilos they want of this same quality of heroin."

I paid him the $10,000 in BNDD money and he gave me the ounce of heroin. The whole deal was being watched by a spotter with binoculars from across the street. After the exchange, the dealer gave me his number in Mexico and told me to call him when I was ready to make a bigger buy. At that point, I was supposed reach into my pocket, pull out a cigarette and light it, signaling the bust. *But I didn't.* That spotter watched as the dealer got into his car and drove away.

· · · · ·

The Last Narc

"What the fuck happened, Berrellez? What happened to the bust signal?" This was John Brown, the case agent in charge of the Tucson unit, and he was pissed.

"It was a very simple buy/bust! What the fuck were you thinking?!"

I told him what I was thinking: That an ounce was nothing. I was thinking that I had gained his trust. And I was also thinking that I believed him when he said he could supply real weight. I knew a hustler when I met one. The dealer I met was the real deal. I knew it. *Why not play it out and bust him for several kilos?*

"It wasn't your call, Berrellez," he said with disdain. "You blew it. Now he's gone and we'll never see him again."

"Of course we will," I said. "He gave me his number. Told me to call him after my Chicago guys tested it."

"You don't have any Chicago guys, Berrellez! You're just a traffic cop who can speak Spanish!"

My blood pressure spiked. I was about to pop off until John Zinter stepped in.

"Hold on," he said. "If this heroin is as good as he says it is, then maybe Hector is right, the guy is the real deal. Let's test it and see, and if it's pure, we'll give him a call."

"If it's even the right number," Brown grumbled.

· · · · ·

Less than a week later, the lab results on the heroin came back. It was 92% pure, which if put on the street would be the best heroin on any coast in America. I called the dealer and told him that my Chicago guys did indeed love it.

"I told you," he said.

We agreed to another deal, this one for two kilos at $250,000 a piece.

• • • • •

"Are you out of your fucking mind, Berrellez? Where are we going to get a 500,000 flash?" It was Brown again.

I hadn't thought about it. The "flash" was the buy money. Typically in drug deals the buyer has to show the flash before the seller shows the drugs. I figured the BNDD would supply it, but Zinter explained that they didn't have that kind of money. I didn't know because we hadn't discussed it, and now it was a problem. As the Tucson unit griped about the whole deal, I made a bold suggestion.

"I'll get him to give it to me without the flash."

Brown rolled his eyes and threw up his hands as if I were the biggest idiot in world. But Zinter studied me carefully.

"You think you can get him to do that, Hector?" he asked.

I did. You can call it ego. Hubris. Whatever. *But I just knew that I could.*

So we planned for another buy/bust, this time with two kilos of pure heroin in play — and no money to buy it.

• • • • •

A couple of weeks later, the deal with the Mexican was set at a hotel on the border in Douglas, Arizona. The Tucson unit along with the BNDD set up a bust team in position to swoop in and make the arrest as soon as I gave the bust signal, again, by lighting a cigarette. The Tucson unit still wasn't certain that a bust would even happen. They didn't believe that the dealer would show up let alone show me the kilos without seeing the money first. I knew otherwise.

I met the dealer in the lobby of the hotel. He was seated at a small table near the corner with a coffee in front of him. As soon as he saw me, he smiled and signaled me over. He shook my hand warmly.

"How are you, Manny?" he asked.

"A little nervous. I hope you're not screwing with me. I really need this deal to go through."

He nodded assuredly before leaning in, as if sharing a secret. "Sit."

And I did.

He looked at me seriously. "Before we do our deal, Manny, I brought a special gift for you." Off my curious look, he slid a small bag of white powder to me. "Do you know what that is, Manny?"

I said no.

"That is cocaine. Very good cocaine. 22 ounces of it. And I'm giving it to you."

I looked at him. He was serious. And he was looking at me with kindness, like my own father had looked at me.

"What you can do, Manny, is you can get some milk sugar, and you can make each of those ounces into two ounces, and then you can sell those 44 ounces for $2,000 each. That's $88,000. I'm giving you this so you can help your mother. Because I think you're a good kid."

"I don't know what to say, sir. *Thank you.*"

He gave me a sincere, appreciative smile and then shifted gears. "Now. About our business. *Did you bring the money?*"

"I did," I said. "It's in my car."

"Okay, Manny. Let's go get it."

I scratched my head, uncertain. "May I see the product first? I'm afraid you're going to rip me off."

The dealer let out a frustrated sigh. "Typically, the money is shown first, Manny." But he picked up the briefcase at his side, put it on his lap and opened it up a crack, just enough for me to see the two kilos of heroin inside. That was good enough for me and we left the lobby for the parking lot.

As the dealer and I walked toward my state-issued undercover police car, I felt a pang of remorse wash over me. In just a short period of time I had bonded with this man and he trusted me. He was showing compassion for the sick mother I didn't have and now I was going to betray him. This would be the first time I would experience such a drastic swing of emotions. I had walked into the lobby of the hotel excited to do my job and bust a drug dealer. Now all I could feel was a deep sense of shame and guilt. *I had lied to him.* Not only was he going to go to jail, he was now going to do even more time thanks to his generosity toward me. I hated myself.

We reached the rear of my sedan. I slipped the key into the trunk and popped it open. There was nothing in it. The dealer looked at me, confused.

"It's empty, Manny. Where is the money?"

Without looking at him I reached into my pocket and pulled out a cigarette, lit it. I turned and met his stare. Though it only lasted moment, it seemed we both understood what was happening simultaneously.

No... He seemed to say.
I'm sorry... I replied.
How could you...?
It's my job...
We heard a dozen policemen storm toward us, one of them yelling, "FREEZE! PUT YOUR HANDS UP! YOU'RE UNDER ARREST!"

• • • • •

Later that night, the whole team got together at a local bar to drink beers and pat each other on the back. I wasn't really in the mood to celebrate but I showed up and tried to pretend I was having a good time. John Brown acted like the mastermind behind the whole case, bragging that he was the one who had turned the informant and orchestrated the bust. One of the other members of the unit interrupted him. "What about Hector? He was right, you know."

Brown scoffed. "Any monkey can buy dope," he said.

Either he didn't know I was there, or didn't care. Either way, I got up and left. On the way out of the bar I passed another officer named Charlie Lugo. He was a good man, a fellow Mexican and a friend. He pulled me aside and said, "Don't worry about it, Hector. They treat us all like that. You did good."

• • • • •

The very next week I was back in my highway patrol office. While I was still feeling pretty bad about betraying the Mexican attorney, the truth was I had a blast on the case. I loved creating "Manny" and going undercover. Now I had to go back out to the interstate and give tickets for drivers going 65 in a 55. Before I left for the day, I received a phone call. It was John Zinter.

"Hector. You did a helluva a job on that case. Great instincts."

"Thank you, John," I said without much enthusiasm.

"Listen, Hector, I know you feel bad. That means you did your job."

"It's still tough. That guy really liked me."

Then Zinter said something that changed not only the way I felt, but my entire view of working undercover. "No he didn't, Hector. *He liked Manny.*"

"Thank you, John," I said, this time with genuine appreciation.

"Now, let me ask you a question. Do you think you'd like to do that full time?"

"I don't know, John. I don't think I like working with the Tucson unit very much."

"Oh. But this isn't for the Tucson unit."

He had my attention.

"The BNDD is being funneled into a new federal department. We're getting a lot of money and more latitude than any other agency in the country. It's going to be rock and roll law enforcement, Hector."

"What's the name of it?" I asked.

"The Drug Enforcement Administration."

I thought about it for a second, then looked at the radar gun on my desk and the stack of speeding tickets I was supposed to give out that day.

"We're not looking for pencil-pushers, Hector," he added. "We want cowboys like you. *You interested?*"

Hmm... *Rock and roll law enforcement? Was I interested?*

"Hell yes I'm interested, John."

Chapter 6

Las tres letras
The Three Letters

Even though she didn't know anything about it, my mother didn't want me to join the DEA. Hell, I didn't know anything about it. It was a brand new wing of our federal law enforcement. She wasn't just worried that I was taking a new job, she knew something I didn't: that I was graduating into a bigger and more dangerous world. This was reinforced to her during a reading she had done for me before I left for academy. My mother was often quiet during our readings, as if she were trying to translate a language she didn't fully understand. I had stopped looking at the cards long ago and learned to just focus on her. My mother's facial expressions and body language were my tarot cards. A raised eyebrow or deep sigh meant something foreboding. The bend of her pursed lips into the slightest of smiles meant a good fortune might be coming my way. But before I left for the academy, I picked up neither such hints from my mother. Her reactions to the cards were nonplussed.

"What do you see, momma?" I asked. And I'll never forget her answer.

"Veo cambio, Memin," she said with a hint of sorrow.
I see change.
"Estás dejando este mundo atrás."

You are leaving this world behind.
"Usted estará en el mundo de los lobos."
You will be in the world of the wolves.

· · · · ·

After 16 weeks of rigorous physical training in combat, memorizing arrest laws, studying drugs, learning the art of evidence gathering and processing — not to mention a 1,000 rounds a day at the range — the DEA gave me a badge, a gun (a brand new Sig Sauer 9mm) and a general directive to "go arrest a bad guy." This is likely a far cry from today's graduating agents, who probably get a laptop and an iPhone. I was assigned as a field agent in Douglas, Arizona, less than three hours from where I grew up in South Tucson.

The first night I reported to my new assignment, my supervisor pulled me into his office and handed me a wad of cash.

"That's $3,000, Berrellez. Your monthly buy money. You need any more, fill out a request."

And that was it. I walked toward my desk and was about to sit down when my supervisor called out to me again.

"What are you doing, Berrellez? Criminals don't walk in here and turn themselves in. Get your ass out there."

I didn't even know what street to go to.

· · · · ·

I began my career going to dive bars and doing tequila shots with every stranger I met in an effort to find informants. I didn't

The Last Narc

know my head from my ass, but I was good with people, and as John Zinter pointed out, I had excellent instincts. Thanks to these instincts, I managed to pick up a pulse of nefarious activities in the area. Douglas, I discovered, was a quietly dangerous city. It may have looked like a sleepy little southwestern town on the outside, but the place was teeming with low-level dealers and criminals who worked both sides of the border.

My first taste of a major bust came by pure luck. I happened to be at my desk one night, probably filling out paperwork for more "buy money" when I received a call from the U.S. Border Patrol. They had just jumped a huge load of marijuana — almost 2,500 pounds. A bunch of agents had been sitting in the darkness watching a section of the border fence when they saw a pick-up truck with a camper shell pull up. A giant of a man stepped out, walked over to the fence and began cutting a huge hole. At that time, the fence was nothing more than chicken wire on sticks. The guy could have used nail clippers. They watched as he snipped the wire, hopped back in his pick-up and drove across the border. As soon as he did, they cut off his truck with their vehicles and surrounded him, ordering him out of the pick-up. The man stepped out — and attacked the nearest agent. Two other agents jumped into the fray and a beating ensued. *For the border agents.* It took all of them to subdue the monster, whose wrists were so big they couldn't even cuff him. Several agents ended up bloodied and one even ended up with a broken collarbone. Somehow they managed to throw him into one of the patrol vans, which doubled as a mobile holding cell. But there was one problem: Nobody wanted to drive the savage to Douglas. That's why they called me.

I made the drive to the desert scene and when I arrived, I saw a huge pile of marijuana and a group of battered patrol agents sitting around licking their wounds. I was DEA now and had to look and act the part. That meant wearing my Randolph aviators despite it being nearly pitch black outside. I parked and stepped out of my sedan like a real badass. I gave a cursory glance to the pile of weed and tried not to look too impressed. For the sake of my sight, I took off my aviators and shook the hand of the agent in charge. The first thing he did was apologize.

"I'm sorry for dragging you out here. But this motherfucker is a beast. We're a little concerned about transporting him."

I was young. And though nobody knew it, I could fight. But there was nothing about me physically that suggested I was a badass. I may have looked like a cowboy, but I was a five foot ten inch middleweight. I looked over at the mobile holding cell with an icy glare before turning back to the agent. "You guys drive the load back to Douglas. I'll take the prisoner." There was a collective gasp of relief from the patrol agents — with a tinge of horror.

"Are you sure?" the agent asked.

He knew that DEA agents drove standard sedans with no cage.

It would just be me, the small man in front of him and that elephantine creature it took all of them to subdue. I nodded. It was too late to take it back. I walked up to the rear of the holding van, pulled out my .45 and said, "Let him out."

The door opened, and six feet three inches and 230 pounds of muscle stepped down from the van. Arms like railroad ties shot out of his white tee. Blue jeans, Tony Lama boots. *What the fuck have I gotten myself into?* There was something else in the man too.

Something I couldn't quite pin down yet because I hadn't been in the field very long. But I had been around this kind of presence before. It was something that alerted my spirit to be on guard. *It was something evil.* I had the urge to cross myself but I held back. With the weight of every border agent's stare upon me, I saddled up.

"*Listen to me, motherfucker. I'm DEA. You're under arrest for smuggling drugs into this country and I'm taking you to jail. So here's the fucking deal. I'm going to drive with one hand on the steering wheel and one hand on my .45 with the barrel pointed at your head. You will keep both of your hands on the dash — and I swear to God, dude, I will kill you if you take them off. I will shoot you if you fuck with me. So don't fucking do anything but stare straight ahead, because if you so much as turn to look at me, I will shoot you in the fucking face and write-off the bullet. Do you understand?*"

The monster looked at me, shrugged and said, "Okay."

If we had computers in our cars back in the day, I might have passed on offering that ride. My uncuffed passenger's name was Hector Fragoso. Though never convicted, he was a known Mexican contract killer whose nickname was "Tombstone." He had been arrested in a variety of assault-related cases. I didn't know the full danger I was in, but *I felt it.*

I made the drive back to Douglas and Fragoso was true to his word, keeping both of his hands on the dash without a word. I kept mine as well, driving with one hand on the steering wheel and one pointing my .45 at his head. Only once was the silence broken when he asked me for a cigarette. I told him he could take one from the pack on the dashboard — but he would have to reach for it in slow-motion. He did. He lit it and said, "Thank you, sir." He was very polite.

When we arrived back at Douglas, all the other agents watched in awe as I ushered the un-cuffed behemoth out of the car and into the booking area. Before I passed him off, the giant turned to me and said, "Hey, thanks for not shooting me in the fucking face."

I nodded and replied, "Thanks for not fucking with me."

The next morning, some U.S. Marshals came to Douglas to pick him up and transport him to Tucson, where the closest U.S. magistrate was based. Later he'd plead guilty to possession of more than a ton of marijuana and was sentenced to five years in federal prison in Safford, Arizona. He was my first official collar.

• • • • •

I didn't hear a thing about Fragoso, or even think about him, for an entire year, until I received a call from the U.S. Marshalls informing me he had escaped from prison. "Well, I'll keep an eye out for him," I said, thinking I would never see the son of a bitch again. Just a few months later, I was having a couple drinks at the flamenco bar in Agua Prieta, Sonora, Mexico, watching the dancing girls, when a bartender came up to me with a frosty cold cerveza and said, *"That guy in the corner just bought you this beer."*

I looked over and there sitting in the corner was a massive dude wearing a cowboy hat, sunglasses and an ear to ear smile beneath them. It was Fragoso — *and he tipped his hat!* We both knew that I had no authority to arrest him in Mexico but it was still my move. I made it a ballsy one. I walked over to Fragoso's table and took the seat right next to him.

"Good afternoon, Agent Berrellez," Fragoso began. "Good to see you again."

"Hello, Mr. Fragoso. I heard you escaped."

He smiled. "More like *vacation.*"

I studied the man. That same feeling I'd had when he stepped down from the van just a year earlier washed over me. *This man is evil.*

"Vacation?" I said. "That's good to hear. So when you going back?"

Fragoso's face went serious. "Actually, I'd like to talk to you about that, agent. Do you have a business card so I might call you when I'm ready to return?"

I looked at the giant. I couldn't believe it. "You serious?" I asked.

Fragoso nodded. He leaned in, a little embarrassed. "I've got syphilis. And I know if I turn myself in, the U.S. government doctors will cure me because they don't want a man with syphilis in the general population of a federal prison."

Fragoso was right. The health care in American prisons was like the Mayo Clinic compared to most Mexican prisons. Fragoso went on to say, rather convincingly, that he just wanted to do his time and move on with his life.

"Please, Agent Berrellez, give me your card and I'll give you a call when I'm ready. I just have a few loose ends to tie up before I go back to prison."

I thought to myself, *well, this is pretty fucking weird...* But I handed him my card.

· · · · ·

Less than a month later, I was working out of my office in Douglas when I received a call. "Hello, Agent Berrellez. Do you remember me?"

It was Fragoso. *How the hell could I forget?*

He told me he was ready to go back to prison. The caveat was that he wanted me to meet him at the border and take him into custody in person. "And why is that?" I asked.

"Because other motherfuckers always fuck with me. And because you are a gentleman, Agent Berrellez."

I sighed. Checked my watch. "When?"

"In one hour at the Douglas border station."

I drove to the port of entry and waited, and sure as shit, exactly one hour later, there comes the gigantic Fragoso, carrying a suitcase like he's going on a cruise. He walked up to me, shook my hand and said, "I'm ready. Let's go."

I didn't even bother to cuff him. I started to give him the *Reader's Digest* version of the speech I gave to him years earlier but he cut me off.

"Yeah, yeah, I know," he said. "You'll put a bullet in my face."

This time the drive to the Douglas station was quite a bit shorter. But with U.S. Marshalls waiting, again I showed up looking like a Mexican super cop, walking in with this wanted monster/fugitive who was carrying his suitcase. Before I handed Fragoso over I said to him, "Good luck, Fragoso. Go do your time, get cured of that nasty disease and change your life."

Fragoso thanked me. Said he would.

The Last Narc

He didn't.

In the years after Fragoso finished his sentence, he became a freelance enforcer and a hitman for the drug cartels. Then in the spring of 1989, he was on the front page of newspapers all over the country. It started with the discovery of five bodies in a shed in Tucson. Three of the men were from Sonora, Mexico and two were from Arizona. All five had been tortured and hogtied, then stabbed to death. The FBI and Tucson homicide named Fragoso the prime suspect and they called me to see if I had any leads on his whereabouts. I didn't have much for them. Remembering the little cold one we shared together years back at the flamenco bar, I suggested they look for him near Agua Prieta. They did and found a ranch nearby that Fragoso had paid for in cash.

When authorities searched the ranch, they didn't find Fragoso. What they found instead was a killing field, a slaughterhouse. They pulled nine bodies from the property's well, using firemen's hooks to fish them out. They pulled another three corpses out of a septic tank. The corpses were so badly decomposed they were fused together, partially skeletal and covered in lime. All of the bodies were horribly mutilated. Even for seasoned homicide cops and feds it was beyond grisly, the stuff of horror films. The female victims had their breasts cut off. The male victims had their penises cut off. All the bodies were missing fingers and limbs. The story made nationwide headlines. Fragoso had even been featured on the hit show *America's Most Wanted*.

I wasn't involved in the ensuing manhunt. But I saw Fragoso's face was all over the news for a week or so. Authorities found him hiding out in a trailer in an isolated desert area near Three Points, Arizona about 30 miles from Tucson. He had dyed his hair red and shaved off his beard and eyebrows. He looked like a clown. The scariest clown you ever saw.

The whole episode made me think about that long ride through the desert, sitting next to the monster. Fragoso had been only two feet away. And I had my .45 pointed at him. *I now knew what I felt then. The man was EVIL.* So I wondered, maybe I should have shot Hector Fragoso right then, right there. I wondered if, had I killed the monster, he wouldn't have been able to torture and kill all those people. And I wondered if I had let my guard down for even one instant, and if Fragoso had been sitting there waiting for such a moment. Finally, I wondered about my own spirit looking up from the bottom of a well. Castrated. Hogtied. Fused to a stranger in a horrific eternal embrace. I wondered about all these things for a long time. Then I remembered what my mother had told me. I was on the other side now. I was *en el mundo de los lobos.*

In the world of the wolves.

Chapter 7

Desnudo en Tejas
Naked in Texas

Not all work at the DEA was guts, bullets and cojones. A lot of it was tedious, boring and repetitious. There was paperwork for everything. This was before the advent of desktops, cell phones and email. Everything had to be written up, proofed and approved before sending out. Agents spent substantial time in the library doing research or in court giving testimony. We put in countless hours on stakeouts that would lead to nothing, or following bogus leads that took us on wild goose chases. There were also those situations of such pure absurdity that no amount of training in any academy could prepare you for. Such was the case of my last and biggest bust before I left Douglas. Like so many of the most interesting cases that comes across the DEA, this one came from a random phone call to my desk. I picked it up.

"Is this agent Berrellez?" a very sweet woman's voice asked.

"It is," I answered.

"My name is Mary and I'm a friend of Bob Montes."

Bob Montes was a paid informant of mine.

"Yes, I know Bob. How can I help you?"

"My husband Carlos is a Mexican Federal Police *comandante* in Mexico City and I know for a fact he's smuggling heroin into Laredo, Texas."

Hmmm, I thought. It sounded like bullshit. We got these calls all the time, some jilted wife who wanted to get her husband in trouble because she was mad at him or something. So I asked her, "Why are you telling me this, Mary?"

"Because the son of bitch is cheating on me with a French actress."

Eureka. I almost hung up the phone. But I paused a moment, took a deep breath and asked in my most annoyed voice, "How is he getting the drugs into Laredo, Mary, and who is he selling them to?"

"Well, I don't know how he's smuggling them in." *Of course.* "But," she added, "I do know who he's selling them too."

"Who?" I asked.

"The police captain of the Webb County narcotics office in Laredo."

· · · · ·

I called my informant.

"Bob. Who the fuck is this Mary lady that called me?"

"Oh, yeah. She's a friend, Hector. Relax. And she's hot as hell."

"I don't give a shit what she looks like. She sounds crazy. Is there even a morsel of truth to what she told me about her husband?"

"Yeah, yeah," Bob said. "He's a big-time heroin dealer from Mexico, dude. I'm helping you out."

The Last Narc

I agreed to meet with them.

•••••

The very next day, I had Bob bring Mary to the DEA headquarters in Douglas. I was working away in my office and the whole place fell silent when they walked in. Bob was not lying. Mary was a supernova. She was about five foot ten, platinum blonde hair, voluptuous body. But as soon as I saw her, I became concerned. Bob wasn't exactly Robert Redford. A woman like Mary could easily have manipulated him. Hell, the lady walking in could have told me the world was flat and I might have believed her. I had them ushered into my office where they both sat down in front of me. After a brief moment of pleasantries, I got to the business at hand.

"So, Mary. Your Mexican *comandante* husband Carlos, who is cheating on you with a French actress, is dealing heroin to a police unit in Laredo, Texas?"

"Yes. And in very large amounts."

"Mary, you know these are very serious allegations?"

"Yes, I do," she said. "What are you going to do about it?"

I didn't like where this was going. The whole thing felt weird to me but that's how the job was sometimes: *weird.* I thought a moment and then spoke honestly. "Listen, Mary. As you may imagine, officially opening a case is a commitment to a lot of time, manpower and money. And I'm not even going to think about it until you provide me with some real proof."

"I understand," she said. "So why don't we just call him right now?"

"Call who?" I asked.

"Lou Munoz. He's the officer in charge in Laredo. He's the one buying the heroin from my husband."

"Uh... Okay."

· · · · ·

I took the pair into our office's soundproof, undercover room where we have a phone with a line that is untraceable. Before Mary dialed the number, she paused, hung up the receiver and gave me a look that I've seen many times from women. *She wanted something.*

"What do you want, Mary?" I asked.

"You know what I want. If I do this, you have to bust the son of a bitch."

Hell, hath no fury.... "Okay. I will."

"What do you want me to say?" she asked.

"Tell him you need money and you have a buyer for him. And that if it works out, you get a cut of the deal."

"Okay," she said, and dialed.

The phone rang for a bit, and then sure as shit, an operator answered, "Sheriff's office."

"Captain Munoz, please," Mary said. She turned to me again and gave me a look,

as if to say, *see, I told you so.*

A second later, the captain picked up. "Munoz."

"Hey, Lou, it's Mary."

"Oh, Mary. How are you?"

"Not good, Lou. I need money. Carlos doesn't give me enough and I was thinking maybe we can help each other."

"And how's that, Mary?" he asked.

"Well, I know what you and Carlos do. And I have a big buyer for you. If I connect you two, will you give me a cut of the deal?"

There was a long silence on the other line until Munoz broke it.

"Mary, you know I don't discuss business over the phone. If you have a buyer for me, you bring him to me here in Laredo. I'll meet with him personally and we'll talk business. If it works out, I'm sure I'll be able to break you off something. How does that sound?"

"That sounds good." As soon as Mary hung up, she looked at me and without missing a beat asked, "Okay, when do we leave?"

• • • • •

About a week later, Mary, Bob and I flew from Arizona to San Antonio to meet with this alleged captain of the Laredo Sheriff's Department. After we picked up our luggage, Captain Munoz met us at our gate and walked us outside to his car — which was a Webb County Sheriff's sedan. He'd left it illegally parked right by the side of the curb with the lights flashing. The guy had balls, I'll give him that.

Once we got in the car, the conversation was innocuous, just small talk about Mary's situation with her husband cheating with the French actress, the weather and such. But when Mary brought up the business we had discussed, again, the captain fell silent.

"I don't want to talk about that. I've rented a hotel room in town. We'll talk there."

The room Munoz rented was at a nearby Best Western. He had already checked in and it was one of those places where you could park right outside your room. We all piled out of the car and he unlocked the door, holding it open for us as we entered. He followed us in, quickly closing it behind him. As soon as it clicked shut, he had his gun drawn and leveled on us.

What the fuck.

"Alright, gang, sorry to do this. But I need you take your clothes off. All of you."

"What the hell are you doing, Lou?" Mary asked.

"I don't know this guy," he said, referring to me. "I wanna make sure he's not a cop and wearing a wire."

"You know I'm not a cop, Lou and neither is Bob," Mary said.

"I don't give a shit. You're all taking your clothes off. And I'm not hearing another word about it."

Okay. More weirdness. But Bob, Mary and I did as we were directed and took off our clothes. Of course I wasn't wearing a wire. No UC ever wore a wire during his first meeting with a potential suspect. Once we were in just our underwear and socks, he still had his gun leveled.

"Uh-uh," he said. "All the way down. Socks and underwear too."

What?

"You could have a wire jammed up your ass for all I know. Take 'em off."

We looked at one another, grumbled about it but I said screw it and took off my socks and briefs. Bob and Mary followed suit. Soon enough, there we were, the three of us standing naked in front of the police captain of Laredo.

"Turn around," Munoz said. We all did a pirouette. Munoz smiled and holstered his gun. "Okay. We're good."

"Oh, no, we're not," I said. "What about you?"

"*What about me?* I am a cop."

"Well, how do we know you're not wearing a wire? You could be taping this whole thing to bust us. You gotta get naked too."

Bob and Mary agreed. Munoz thought about it, shrugged, then took off his clothes. Now all of us were naked, standing their staring at each other, all wondering *what the fuck*. Munoz did a pirouette of his own, showing us that he was clean. When he was done he looked at me and said, "Okay, *now can we talk business?*"

This was the most bizarre situation I had ever been in. As absurd as it was, it was also very tense. Then I looked at Mary, who really was a knockout. She looked like she stepped out of the pages of *Playboy* or something. "Well, now that we're all naked, who's going to fuck who first?" I asked.

We all started laughing, which is exactly the effect I wanted. When we settled, Munoz began.

"So who are you? And how long you been in the business?"

I told him my fake name and alias. I carried a full set of false identification at the time, so that was no problem. I had everything: driver's license, credit cards. Munoz took down all of my information.

"You know why I'm doing this, don't you?" he asked.

"Of course," I said. "You're going to check me out."

"Damn right I am. I want to know right now if you have an arrest record. *Do you?*"

"I got busted for dealing marijuana in Chicago."

"You connected?"

"I am. Chicago syndicate," I said, which was another name for the Italian mob.

"And what kind of quantity can your people handle?"

"Multiple kilos. I'll take whatever you have."

Munoz smiled at the possibility. "Okay. I'm going to run your name to make sure you're not lying to me. If it clears, we'll do business together."

"Sounds good to me," I said.

We stood there for a long, awkward moment. Because, after all, we were still naked.

· · · · ·

A couple of weeks passed since that strange first meeting and I still hadn't heard from the captain, but I wasn't concerned. I made sure my alias' arrest record was in the database. I had given him a safe line to call before we left Laredo. The only calls I got were from Mary. *Did he call…? Did he call…?* Naturally, she was the type of woman who was very accustomed to getting her way and getting it quickly. After about the 50th time she called me at the office, I finally had to dress her down.

"Mary. No, he hasn't called. Some drug deal takes time. So please, don't call me again."

"How long?" she asked.

"How the hell do I know? Could be months or even a year. You might have to accept the fact that he'll never call. Do you understand?"

"I guess so," she said disappointedly, then hung up.

A moment later, as if on cue, my phone rang again. This time, from the safe line.

"Hello?" I said.

"Manny, you son of a bitch. It's Lou from Laredo. You ready to rock and roll?"

· · · · ·

I went solo to my next visit in Laredo. When I arrived, Munoz was there to greet me.

He was dressed in his sheriff's department uniform and picked me up in his marked car. As soon as he started driving I said, "You're not taking me back to the fucking hotel to get naked, are you?"

He laughed. "Not today, Manny."

It was a good thing too. Because *I was wearing a wire.* And this time as we drove, we talked business. Munoz told me he was getting his heroin direct from the best lab in Sinaloa, Mexico and that it was 90% pure. He quoted a price of $250,000 per kilogram. I nodded my head like it was the greatest fucking deal in the world. As was my typical modus operandi in these buy/busts, I had agreed to purchase a sample of the heroin from the captain. If it was as good as he said, I promised my people would do a multi-kilo deal.

I thought maybe the captain would drive me to some dive bar or back-alley haunt to do the sample deal but I couldn't have been more wrong. The ballsy son of a bitch drove me right to the Sheriff's Department headquarters in Laredo. Not only did he take me inside the building, he introduced me to every cop in the place, including narcs and vice guys. They shook my hand and were nice as hell to me. Texas, right? Munoz led me to the drug section of their headquarters where all these long-haired undercovers were hanging out — and he introduced them to me as well. As we proceeded on, he leaned in and confided, "Two of those dudes are DEA."

"No shit?" I said.

"Yeah, but they're cool."

Man, this case kept getting weirder and weirder.

Munoz eventually took me into his private office, which he had because he was the captain. I thought, *Is this motherfucker going to give me the heroin right here in his office in the narcotics unit of the Sheriff's Department?* Sure enough, he closed the door, went into his desk and came out with a zippered bag. "There you go Manny. Go ahead and open it up." I opened the bag and inside were six ounces of heroin. I made a big show of examining it, feeling its viscidity, smelling it. All the while Munoz babbled on about how great it was and how much money my Chicago connections were going to make selling it. And of course, this was all being recorded.

Once I pulled the zipper closed, he said, "Okay, you got the cash?" When I laid the money on his desk, he didn't count it. He just scooped it up and threw it in a drawer. "All right. Let's go party."

• • • • •

I have to give it to Captain Lou Munoz. He was a man of his word and party we did. We spent the rest of the day palling around Laredo, doing dozens of tequila shots. I had a blast and the two of us got along famously. He even took me home to meet his wife and family.

The cherry on top was a late night visit to a place called the Godfather Inn, which was owned by a red-headed Chinese Mexican. No shit. It was truly one of the oddest places I'd ever been in. It made Studio 54 look like a Tuesday night at the Rotary Club. There were strippers next to businessmen sitting with cops around gangsters. On stage, a horrible rock band was butchering the Stones. It was also a place where Munoz was treated like a king. The red-headed Chinese Mexican gave us a private table near the dance floor and almost everyone in the place stopped by to shake his hand. Among those who paid their respects were several of the undercover cops I had met at the precinct — and they didn't seem too happy with me. One of them even leaned in menacingly and warned Munoz, "Cap, I don't like this dude. What the fuck is he doing here?"

"He's with me and we're doing business," Munoz said.

"He doesn't look cool to me."

Munoz studied me a moment and repeated the concern.

"He thinks you're not cool, Manny," he said to me.

"Yeah?" I said. "Well, I don't give a fuck what he thinks."

I got out of my seat and walked up onto the stage. The band's lead singer approached.

"What are you doing, dude?" he asked.

"Gimme a guitar. Let's jam."

The singer looked at me sideways. "What are you thinking?"

"La Bamba."

"That tune don't rock, dude."

"The way I play it, it does,."

He looked at his bandmates, shrugged and they handed me a guitar. I threw it over my shoulder, strummed it a second then stepped up to the microphone.

"This is for that motherfucker that doesn't think I'm cool." I nodded over to my table.

One, two, three...

I went into La Bamba.

And we rocked the place.

• • • • •

Later that night I was taken back to my hotel by a drunk Captain Munoz — still driving his marked sheriff's sedan.

"Man, I like you, Manny," he said.

"I like you too, Lou."

"You ain't like those DEA motherfuckers."

"Why do you say that?" I asked.

"Because you were at that bar with all those beautiful bitches, playing your guitar and you didn't even give a damn. Those DEA guys will fuck anything."

"I'm from Chicago, dude," I proudly said. "These Laredo chicks don't do shit for me." Munoz laughed. "We gonna make a lot of money together, Manny."

"Hell yeah, we are, Lou."

I smiled and stumbled out of his sedan. As he drove away, I felt a genuine affection for the man. I would end up busting poor Captain Lou Munoz for trying to sell me five kilos of heroin. But never in my career would I ever have such a fun time doing it.

Chapter 8

Ringside

Beginning in the mid-1970s and up through the early '80s, two brothers in Douglas, Arizona by the names of Ray and Joe Borane amassed a fortune in real estate through drug smuggling, money laundering and graft. Together, they were a part of the Douglas/Auga Prieta drug cartel and worked in partnership with one of Northern Mexico's most notorious kingpins, Francisco Rafael Camarena. This was not known when I was working in Douglas. While many of us in the law enforcement community believed the two brothers were most likely dirty, there had never been any proof. One reason for this lack of evidence was the fact that the two brothers literally ran Douglas. Joe Borane was the Chief of Police before he became its magistrate. His brother Ray was a prolific fundraiser and built statewide political alliances. He had some political aspirations himself and wanted to be mayor of Douglas. The problem was, Douglas already had a mayor. And not only was Alberto Rodriquez the mayor of Douglas, he was also one of the Borane's most vociferous political enemies. Brother Joe's solution to this problem was simple: *have Rodriquez killed.*

The plan for murdering the mayor of Douglas was revealed to me by one of my informants who told me that Joe Borane and his lieutenant, Dale Lehman, had approached him about contracting the assassination. This put me in a tough spot. The Borane family was very powerful in and around Cochise County, Arizona. The brothers' father had served in the Immigration and Naturalization Service with Bob Iman, who was my direct supervisor at the DEA. So instead of reporting the assassination plot to my supervisor, Iman, I went around him and passed the information to the FBI without his knowledge or authorization.

This was a huge tactical error in judgement. The Boranes were so politically connected that the FBI's investigation went nowhere. And when my supervisor Frank Iman found out about it, he was enraged.

"Berrellez, Goddamit! I should kick your ass for being so stupid!"

Unfortunately, Iman was right. I was a company man and I should have followed protocol. I apologized all over hell, but Iman still gave me an unsatisfactory performance evaluation on my annual job review. I was placed on six-month probation to be fired, and as further disciplinary action for this transgression, I was transferred to the DEA's Los Angeles Field Division.

Yes, I was sent to Los Angeles as "punishment."

• • • • •

The city of angels was an undercover's dream back in the early '80s. Hell, it probably still is today. Los Angeles is an odd amalgam of surf and street cultures, a nexus of urban life, industry and entertainment. Sacramento may be the state's political capital, but it's Los Angeles that drives its culture. At the center of that culture is the glitz and glamour of Hollywood. Any one of these factors would create an environment fertile for drug use and activity. *But all of them combined?*

Aside from the area's culture, L.A.'s ties to the aviation industry made it the perfect place for drug dealing. With 15 of the 25 largest aerospace companies in the world in Southern California, planes, airstrips and hangars were plentiful. The city's location was equally ideal. Dope-rich Mexico and Latin America, a logistical nightmare for the East Coast smuggler, was a literal jump. And with access to Pacific routes through Hawaii, Asia could be in play as well. The world was wide open for the taking. In short, L.A. was a perfect, target-rich environment where I could sprout my wings as an agent. So I did. Stinging from what I perceived to be a demotion after my Douglas appointment, I was hell-bent on proving my superiors wrong. I did this by living my undercover life just over the edge. I had dialed up my "Manny" alter-ego into a legitimate gangster and flamboyant playboy who would throw money at anyone willing to deal. It was probably one of the stupidest ploys an undercover could ever use. Attention might be a good thing in Los Angeles, but it's a bad thing in the underbelly of the drug world. One wrong move and I could have easily gone from drinking champagne at the Beverly Hilton to getting shot in the face and dumped in a ghetto alley off Crenshaw Boulevard in the space of half an hour. Thing is, I didn't care. There wasn't an assignment or a buy/bust I would pass up. It didn't matter how glamorous or how dangerous the case was. It didn't matter how much or how little dope was at stake. I just wanted to make busts. So overzealous was I in my crusade against every low-life dealer in the drug game, I once even arrested a dog. Seriously.

There had been a "blind pig" on the East Side of Los Angeles that was, in reality, a narco bar. It may have passed itself off as a "private social club" but it was owned and operated by mid-level dealers with ties to the Guadalajara Cartel. It was in one of those dumps around Boyle Heights that had no name or address. Even if one were to stumble onto it by accident there was absolutely no admittance unless you were Mexican and you were vouched for. I had been introduced into the place by a criminal informant. I flipped and he arranged a buy/bust of a Columbian dealer who called himself "El Chavo," the kid.

Usually, when planning a buy/bust as an undercover, there is a grace period when you have to watch every person that comes into your orbit very closely. In the drug game everyone has an angle or agenda. Everyone wants to know *what you can do for them*. Your job as a UC is to find the biggest fish and make it known through third parties or passing conversations *that you can offer what they need*. In the academy this is known as the "avenue of approach." You find out what a potential target needs and you figure out a way to fill it. In other words, most of the time, being a UC means observing, calculating, thinking laterally. But this wasn't who I was at the time. I just wanted to bust people. It didn't even matter to me that I hadn't met El Chavo yet. I would have my undercover partner Billy Terrazas with me. I was strapped. *What could go wrong?*

One step into the narco bar and that question was answered. The place was a drug dealer's paradise, pulsating with action. Air thick with marijuana smoke, a *norteño* band blaring *narcocorrido* music and a dozen half-naked girls dancing on stage. Cocaine was everywhere. On the tables. On the bar. In the ashtrays. And everyone in the entire room was either openly dealing, openly

The Last Narc

buying or openly using. Aside from having more characters than a Tarantino movie, the bar even had a pet: a stoned, mangy looking dog that paced about like a sentry, growling at whoever crossed its path. Yes, it was a drug-dealer's paradise. But it was also an *undercover's dream.*

A pair of Mexican goons approached us.

"Get wide," one of them said, which was his was his way of telling us we were to be frisked.

"Fuck you," I said. "You don't know us."

I opened my jacket to show off my gun before breezing past him. I couldn't see Billy's reaction but I'm sure it was something like, *oh shit.* I had been to these types of places in Mexico. They're not for tourists. You have to look and act like a genuine badass. If you look like someone that can be fucked with, *someone will.*

Billy and I met up with my informant and we posted up at a table right in the center of it all. We ordered some beers and waited for El Chavo as we listened to the *narcocorrido* music, which is a whole world unto itself. *Narcocorrido* is a folk-music genre that tells the stories of drug lords, arrests, shootouts and betrayals. They're like *drug lord ballads.* Most of the time, a narco trafficker will commission such a song as a way to immortalize himself, sometimes paying millions of dollars. But such a commission comes with a risk. Singing about the exploits of one drug kingpin will surely offend another. There is a long list of *narcocorristos* all throughout Mexico who have been brutally killed for their craft, which is probably why the *norteño* band who was playing kept it generic.

Todo esta bien contralado senores hagan conciensia!
Ahora que ya tomo el mando el señor Tony Tormenta!

Everything is well under control, be aware people!
Now that Mr. Tony Tormenta is in charge!

It didn't take long for El Chavo to appear. He was a short, stocky Colombian who looked like he spent a lot of money trying to look better than he was, donning an all-white, linen leisure suit with black cowboy boots. My informant had vouched for me as a significant dealer who could move a lot of weight. But as El Chavo squared me up, he didn't act too impressed. Without saying a word he reached into his pocket, pulled out a little baggie of coke and arrogantly flung it me, bouncing it off my chest.

"Escama," he said, which is translated as "scaley" but was implied to mean pure and crystalline. "And I got a shit-ton more where that came from."

My temperature rose. Billy glanced at me with pleading eyes, hoping I wouldn't make trouble. He watched as I reached into my jacket, pulled out my money-clip and drew a one dollar bill. I crumbled it up and flung it at El Chavo, bouncing it off his chest.

He stood in stunned silence.

"What the fuck is that?" he asked.

"You give me this bullshit ounce and tell me you got way more just like it?" I said. "So there, I gave you a dollar. I got a ton more where that came from too."

There was more silence, until El Chavo's face bent into a wide smile.

"I like this motherfucker," he said.

And we made a deal for 300 kilos right there. It would be a "key exchange." El Chavo would have his people retrieve the coke from one car while I had Billy retrieve the money from ours. Once we confirmed the money and dope on the scene, El Chavo and I would simply swap keys to the cars.

Though we had originally planned for just the buy/bust with El Chavo in the parking lot of the narco bar, as I looked around the place, watching everyone go about their criminal business — *and loving it* — I changed the plan. I wanted more. *I wanted to arrest everybody.* Before I sent Billy away to drive around the block for 30 minutes, I told him to call the ADNARC unit of the LAPD and tell them we request backup and a full-on raid of the place. ADNARC was the department's "advanced" narcotic team and I had worked with their captain quite a bit and liked him. They were the best. And they were also a lot like me. *They lived for this shit.*

• • • • •

Less than 45 minutes later, El Chavo's driver returned with the coke and Billy "returned" with the money. We executed the buy with El Chavo and afterwards, on my signal, we hit the place with a classic Hollywood-style bust, bursting through the doors badges out and guns a-blazing.

"FREEZE! DEA! EVERYONE DOWN! HANDS WHERE WE CAN SEE THEM!"

I wish I could say there was chaos. Typically when we blew through the door with our guns and badges, you braced for the worst. Sometimes suspects would run for the exits. Others would dive for cover. You would hear glass breaking, screaming, sometimes even gunfire. You know, all the shit you usually associate with raids.

Not so at the narco bar.

As soon as we burst into the place, there was a collective gasp of shock as if it had to be some kind of mistake, like we had been given a wrong address or something. It pissed me off.

"THIS IS A RAID, GODDAMMIT!" I screamed. "YOU ARE ALL UNDER ARREST!"

And I didn't mean it in the pejorative. *I wanted to arrest everybody.* The captain from the ADNARC unit looked at me curiously. "Arrest everyone, Hector?"

"ARREST EVERYONE!" I yelled. "ARREST THE BARTENDER! ARREST THE DOOR GUY! ARREST THE DANCING GIRLS! ARREST THE MUSICIANS! THE DISHWASHERS AND EVERYONE ELSE IN THIS GODDAMN PLACE!"

They weren't the most reasonable orders, but they were followed and in a matter of moments everyone in the whole place was being ushered out in cuffs, leaving nothing but that mangy, stoned dog.

"What about the dog?" someone asked.

"ARREST HIM TOO!" I snapped. "HE'S AN ACCOMPLICE TO ALL OF THIS SHIT!"

And so they put the mangy mutt right in the paddy wagon with the other suspects. (We ended up letting him go.)

Everyone looked at me like I was crazy and they were probably right. That's just the way I was when I was first transferred to Los Angeles. Thankfully, I managed to mellow out with a little time on the job. But it wasn't until the beginning of 1983 when I really started to learn the trade.

・・・・・

Anyone who knows the history of the War on Drugs knows the name Thomas "Tootie" Reese. At the time, the great majority of cocaine and heroin being sold in black communities across the country was imported and distributed by two major black drug kingpins. As the head of a drug organization based in Harlem called the Council, Leroy Nicholas "Nicky" Barnes controlled the East Coast. Controlling the West Coast from his base of operations in South Central Los Angeles was Tootie Reese. Between the two of them, it was said that Reese was the one who was "untouchable." And with good reason. Reese was as cautious as he was smart. He rarely traveled, never talked business with strangers and kept a fiercely loyal inner coterie. He was allegedly bankrolled into the drug game in the mid-1970s by famous boxing promoter Don King and began taking Los Angeles one neighborhood at a time. By the early 1980s Reese was legend. He was driven around in a custom-built Cadillac with 24-karat gold rims. He never left his house with less than $170,000 in cash, what he called his "walkin' around money."

The L.A. Division of the DEA had been after Tootie Reese for several years at that point and the lead agents on the case were two of the very best black undercover agents in the DEA: Charlie Brown and Simeon Green. Those brothers were something else. Dressed to work undercover, they looked like they stepped right off the set of *Super Fly* — big afros, leather pants, white silk suits with matching hats that came with bright pink feathers. They looked like millionaire pimps, which was exactly the image they were after.

By getting close to a couple of Reese's lieutenants and befriending his bodyguards, Charlie and Simeon had successfully infiltrated Reese's organization. But for the next six or seven months, their investigation stalled. They just couldn't get close enough to Tootie. They were very subtle, but whatever trick they tried, it didn't work. He would rarely meet with them and when he did he would never talk business, despite the fact that they were posing as heroin dealers with great connections in Mexico. We had hoped their supposed Mexican connections would interest Tootie because his sources for heroin were all tied to Asia. (Tootie was getting China white heroin. Charlie and Simeon were posing as wholesalers of Mexican black tar heroin, which is a lot less expensive than China white.) But Tootie was smart and he kept his distance — even if they were friends with his lieutenants and bodyguards.

Every month, we'd have a meeting at the L.A. Division where Charlie and Simeon would update us on the progress of the investigation. And every month at this meeting, we were hearing the same chorus: *We just can't get next to Tootie.*

Finally, at a meeting late that summer of 1983, I came up with an idea.

"How about we fool him," I said.

"How?" they asked.

"Look, you guys are posing as real heroin dealers with connections in Mexico, right?"

They nodded.

"Then why don't you do a real drug deal with your real Mexican connection, Manny from Sinaloa?" I pointed to myself as if it were the greatest fucking idea ever. They looked at me like I had just spoken in Yiddish.

"He don't trust us," said Simeon. "What makes you think he'll trust you?"

"Yeah," Charlie chimed in. "And how does that fool Tootie anyway?"

"We don't have to fool Tootie," I said. "We only have to fool *his bodyguards*."

Simeon understood. He smiled at me. "Spell it for us, brother."

• • • • •

The plan was for Charlie and Simeon to approach Tootie's bodyguards with an opportunity. They had a major drug deal going down with their Sinaloa Cartel connection and they needed some extra muscle for security, for which they would offer them $5,000 a piece for the night.

This was easy money for the bodyguards. There was no doubt that Tootie was paying his guys well, but $5,000 for maybe two hours of work would never be passed up — especially for guys who came from the streets. We also knew that not only would Tootie's bodyguards take the job, they would immediately run back to Tootie and tell him all about it. That was just the nature of the drug game. All players in the drug game operated on reputation, word of mouth and notoriety. We wanted to make sure when Tootie got wind of this deal with the Mexicans, he'd be begging to get into business with them. To do this, we had to make damn sure to stage a deal that blew the top off any of the deals Tootie's crew had been accustomed to.

First, we would use real money: three million in cash. No "Chicago flash" where the authentic bills were on top and the rest was counterfeit. And we would use grade A Mexican black tar heroin that did, in fact, come from Sinaloa. The DEA had made a significant bust at the border a few months earlier. We took the kilos straight from the evidence locker where it was still shrink-wrapped with the cartel's iconic symbol: a variation of the *Jolly Roger* sign with a colorful skull and a pair of AK-47s for crossbones.

I also had to take my "Manny from Sinaloa" persona even higher. There is not merely a small gap between a mid-level drug hustler and a legitimate drug dealer, there is a dimension. Any character who has the weight to sell $3 million of heroin and the power to move it must look and act the part. I was more than up to the task. By now I had carefully studied the habits, mannerisms and backgrounds of every major drug lord throughout Mexico and Central America. I knew how they walked, talked, dressed and spoke. But just as important as dressing and acting the part was surrounding yourself with a crew who also looked like the real deal. You need guys who look paranoid as fuck, smell like back-country *pistoleros* and act like serious badasses to watch your back and stand by your side when the drug deal goes down. For this, I recruited Hispanic undercover DEA agents. Back in those days, the Hispanic undercover guys looked like outlaws. They had long hair, beards and dressed like real Sinaloan Cowboys — Western shirts and denim jeans with hub-cap sized belt buckles. They also carried real AK-47s. I added a few notable accoutrements as well: ostrich skinned boots and gold Rolexes. Authentic *pistoleros* had a thing with boots. The odder the skin, the more pride they took in them. And they always wore gold watches, which were usually either gifts from their drug lord employer or lifted off the wrist of one of their many victims. By the time I finished putting together my crew, the best costume and makeup people at Paramount Pictures couldn't have made them look any more real.

The coup de grâce of our ambitious plan was where we would set it. We decided to do it at one of the best and most prestigious hotels in Los Angeles: in a $1,500 a night executive suite at the Beverly Hilton.

· · · · ·

I had been a part of "show deals" in the past. They almost always proceeded without incident while also serving their purpose — to put on a show for a suspect in an investigation. These deals are used as an invaluable tool for an undercover to gain standing within the party he's investigating. They can also be quite exciting. As an undercover, it's often thrilling to immerse yourself in your character and play the scenario up — even to have fun with it to a certain degree. This is especially true during the preparation and buildup. Once the moment of the deal arrives, any excitement, thrill or fun goes out the window. It's replaced with anxiety, nervousness and sometimes straight out fear. Such was the case in the staged deal with Charlie, Simeon and their hired bodyguards. It was as terrifying as any real deal I had ever done. And with good reason — *it was too real.*

There comes a point in any undercover deal when a dark reality settles and everyone involved asks themselves the same question: *Do I trust these motherfuckers?* In every situation, the answer on both sides of the equation is an emphatic *no*.

Ten minutes into our deal, every player in our suite at the Hilton had just asked themselves that same question and came to the same conclusion. When that moment comes, you don't know if someone is going to lose their cool and start firing. What worries you even further is that someone just might be *you*.

On one side of the suite, I stood with a half-dozen of the baddest looking Mexicans you could imagine. On the other side stood Charlie, Simeon and four of Tootie Reese's most hardened bodyguards. On the table between us were a dozen kilos of black tar heroin and an open suitcase with $3 million in real cash. Everybody in the room was openly armed with loaded semi-automatic weapons. It was insanely tense.

Charlie and Simeon were terrific as the buyers. During a drug deal, neither side can ever appear satisfied. Both act as if they have made innumerable concessions to facilitate the transaction. Even after the dope and money are exchanged, there's never a mutual celebration. Dealers take the money in stride. Buyers take the dope and run. In most cases, the entire deal takes less than 20 minutes. Charlie, Simeon and "Manny" from Sinaloa needed only 15.

After the deal, Charlie and Simeon left with the heroin while I stayed in the suite with my crew and the three million. Less than two hours later we met back at DEA headquarters and all the cash and heroin was back in the DEA safes. *And Tootie's bodyguards?* They were running back to tell Tootie about this $3 million black

The Last Narc

tar heroin deal they'd just seen go down with their own eyes — and about the major supplier from Sinaloa named Manny.

· · · · ·

A few days later, Tootie sent word through his bodyguards to Charlie and Simeon that he wanted to meet. They knew exactly what he wanted to meet about. He wanted to sell them some China white. Here's where the art of being an undercover comes into play. The guys would have to tell him in no uncertain terms, *"Go fuck yourself. We don't need you anymore."* And that's exactly what Simeon and Charlie did.

"Man, you wouldn't give us the time of day when we asked to meet with you over and over again. But now that you know we're for real you want to do business? Fuck you, Tootie.'"

Yes. They told Tootie Reese to fuck off, which is usually not a good move for most people. However, it is always a very good move when you're undercover. This is something Charlie and Simeon understood. As a UC, you never want to seem too eager to make a deal. You have to be the one playing hard to get. Drug dealers like Reese are accustomed to getting what they want. And when they can't, they're the ones who start to press.

Like clockwork, a couple of weeks go by and Tootie again passes word to Charlie and Simeon that he wants to do business. But there is a caveat to his proposition, one we all knew was coming. *Tootie wants to meet Manny as well.*

· · · · ·

It was late summer 1983 and there was a world championship prizefight coming up at Caesar's Palace in Las Vegas, the big rematch between Aaron Pryor and Alexis Arguello. Tootie told Charlie and Simeon that he had seats to the fight and wanted to invite them as his personal guests — but of course, they had to bring Manny as well. Naturally, we agreed.

We received five-star V.I.P. treatment all the way. Don King, who was promoting the fight, personally sent a limousine to drive us from L.A. to Vegas. We stayed in luxury suites at Caesar's Palace, and the night of the fight, King took us into the dressing rooms to meet the fighters. We watched the fight from ringside, first row, and every time I saw a TV camera pointed my way I made sure it got a good view of me, because I knew all the DEA guys I worked with and my family back home were watching that fight. They all loved boxing.

After the fight, Tootie pulled me aside and said he wanted to speak with me alone. We arranged to meet the next day at an upscale restaurant on the Las Vegas Strip. At the meeting, he made a lucrative offer to buy Mexican black tar heroin straight from me and cut Charlie and Simeon out of the profits.

"Hell no, man," I said. "I don't know you. You could be a black undercover DEA agent for all I know."

Tootie got offended. "Do you know who the fuck I am? I'm Tootie fucking Reese. I'm the fucking man. Ask anybody."

"Sorry, dude. I'm from Sinaloa. I don't know you. I can't sell to you directly."

Tootie couldn't believe his ears. "You're really not going to sell to me?"

"No, I'm not selling to you. You gotta get the shit from my guys. I'll give them a good price and tell them to take care of you, but you got to buy from them."

He started buying Mexican black tar heroin from Charlie and Simeon. They built a rock solid case and we nailed him on multiple felony counts for buying and selling massive amounts of heroin. He was sentenced to 80 years.

· · · · ·

Tootie Reese was careful and he was smart. But in the end, like all of them, *he was greedy*. For a guy like Tootie, there's no such thing as having enough money. He always wanted more, and that insatiable greed is what got him busted. That was his weakness. That's how we took him down. That's how we take them all down. But the thing about the drug game is that when one Tootie Reese goes down, another one pops up. It's a never-ending cycle endemic to the criminal drug-dealing world. However, something strange and dangerous was happening in the L.A. drug scene. It seemed as if overnight, we weren't just chasing after one Tootie Reese at a time. We were chasing after dozens, in every neighborhood, on every block. It all began when I started hearing about a new ring of traffickers who were flooding the streets of South Central Los Angeles with cocaine, selling kilos at bargain prices.

It was around this time that I discovered my first clues into the existence of a dark alliance between U.S. officials and Mexican drug cartels. Little did I know that this was the same alliance that would soon lead to the abduction, torture and murder of a fellow agent that would shock the country and rock the DEA to its very core.

Chapter 9

The Day the DEA Stood Still

There's not an active DEA agent or any federal agent, for that matter, who doesn't know exactly where they were on Thursday, February 7th, 1985. That was the day our Kennedy got shot. While the DEA had lost agents in the past to the dangers of the job, this was the first time in federal law enforcement history that anybody had dared to break the unwritten rule that even the most vile drug lords and cartels had always taken to heart: *Never touch an American agent.*

I was still on assignment in Los Angeles and I remember being at the gym when the news broke. I was on the treadmill, not paying full attention to the television in front of me, when all of a sudden fellow agent Enrique "Kiki" Camarena's face appeared above the headline, "Agent Abducted." I literally froze in my tracks.

Though American authorities responded swiftly to the kidnapping, clues to Kiki's whereabouts and who was involved were not forthcoming. Until then, the idea of even the most brazen of cartels kidnapping a U.S. agent was unimaginable. This was new ground for the DEA and even weeks after Kiki went missing, we were still in the dark. But we were determined. So much so that President Ronald Reagan even shut down the U.S.-Mexico border until we found him. Finally, and tragically, almost a month after his abduction, Kiki's body was discovered buried in a shallow grave outside Guadalajara. He had been brutally tortured, severely beaten and sodomized with a broom handle. His abductors had even injected him with lidocaine to keep him alive during the torture. He was only 37 years old.

• • • • •

Kiki Camarena's accomplishments as well as his legacy cannot be overstated. He worked in Mexico at the very pinnacle of America's War on Drugs, in one of the most hostile places in the world, yet despite the overwhelming corruption that crippled almost every investigation he spearheaded, he somehow managed to do his job: *He did damage to the world's largest cartel.* He did so much damage that he was killed for it, which is the reason, to this day, there is still a picture of him hanging on the wall in every DEA office in the world.

• • • • •

Kiki's abduction, torture and murder was the match that ignited the modern American War on Drugs. The world waited for a U.S. response that would be a bellwether for the geopolitical narco-policy that still exists today. Even now, more than 30 years later, Kiki's murder pulses in international political quarters as well as in the hearts of lawmen on both sides of the border. So much so that the case and its key players remain the subject of folk songs throughout the Americas. It has even been adopted into modern-day pop-culture through the enormously popular Netflix series *Narcos: Mexico.*

Every agent I knew and worked with volunteered to go down to Mexico to help in the subsequent investigation of Kiki's murder. DEA headquarters had never fielded so many requests for transfer from agents. The outpouring of offers to assist in the case wasn't limited to just the DEA either. Hundreds of FBI officials, border agents and narc cops on both sides of the border volunteered their services. Even average citizens tried to help. Volunteer militias sprouted up, search parties were organized and private investigators tried to solve the incident on their own.

Kiki's murder was something of a seismic event for me. He was not just a colleague. Like me, he was also a combat veteran. Like me, he was also a faithful, devoted husband and father. And like me, he was also Hispanic. While Kiki and I never actively worked together, I had confided with him over the years about several cases. We were kindred spirits and I liked him. He was one of the good guys. After he was murdered, I was thrust into a state of depression. I saw myself in him. It could have just as easily been me working in Mexico. Whatever situation Kiki found himself in, there was no doubt in my mind that the same thing could have happened to me. Instead of being grateful that I was working on the U.S. side of the border, *I felt guilty that I wasn't where the real War on Drugs was being fought.* Kiki was a true soldier in this war. He was on the front lines. I was just a tourist who got to play dress up.

· · · · ·

The guilt I harbored for not being assigned in Mexico was compounded by my superiors' refusal to put me on the Camarena case. I firmly believed there was nobody in the agency better suited for the investigation. I begged my superiors to send me to Mexico but my pleading fell on deaf ears. So I would just do as I was told. I was, after all, a company man.

What I perceived as my diminishment by my superiors manifested something very dangerous in me. It was a danger rarely mentioned in the circles of law enforcement. It was not a physical danger, *it was a moral danger.* Most people rightfully point out the physical dangers of work in law enforcement. Yes, you can get shot at. Yes, you can get killed. Most agents of law enforcement are constantly surrounded by this physical danger — especially undercover agents. But there also comes a point when agents can *become the danger.* Not just to criminal suspects at large or their partners, but more importantly *to themselves.* Drinking to numb pain is a moral danger. Sex outside of a committed relationship is a moral danger. And the allure of easy money is a moral danger. All of these moral dangers are omnipresent on the job and any one of them can kill an agent just as easily as a bullet from a gunman. These dangers are all triggered by the same feelings of insecurity I felt at the time — *that I wasn't good enough.* No matter how many drug dealers I busted or how many bad guys I shot, I just wasn't good enough. I was still that small-town cop from South Tucson and as I had been reminded early in my career, *any monkey can buy dope.*

• • • • •

While my feeling of inadequacy would contribute to the moral dangers of the job, it also made me a damn good agent. It gave me a chip on my shoulder and an ax to grind. Ultimately, it would also get me what I wanted. Because after two years of raising hell in L.A., in 1987, I would finally get half of my wish. I wasn't going to work on the Camarena case, which still was under investigation, but I was going to Mexico. And I was going right into what was the center of biggest turf war in the history of illegal narcotics. It was the most dangerous place in the world, a place even its own residents called *infierno*. It was also home to the biggest and most powerful drug cartel in the world.

I was going to Guadalajara.

PART TWO

BAPTISM

In the deeps are the violence and terror of which psychology has warned us. But if you ride these monsters deeper down, if you drop with them farther over the world's rim, you find what our sciences cannot locate or name, the substrate, the ocean or matrix or ether which buoys the rest, which gives goodness its power for good, and evil its power for evil, the unified field: our complex and inexplicable caring for each other, and for our life together here. This is given. It is not learned.

–Annie Dillard, Teaching a Stone to Talk

Chapter 10

Bienvenido a Mexico
Welcome to Mexico

One of the troubles of being a DEA agent in places like Los Angeles was that even though my salary may have been at a decent GS-13 level, the money didn't go very far. The cost of living — especially with wife and child — really limited where I could live and what kind of lifestyle I could give to my family. As a man who wanted to provide for them in the best possible way, this hurt me. Compounding the feeling of inadequacy was the fact that while I was at work, I got to live and act like a rock star. I drove fast cars, wore expensive clothes and hung out with some of Tinseltown's wealthiest. I'm not going to lie, it's not always easy rolling out of some hot Hollywood nightclub in a convertible Corvette, wearing enough gold and ice to pay for my daughter's college education only to turn it in, drive back home in my lousy Pontiac and then have to cut my lawn in Riverside. All of that changed when I was promoted to Resident Agent in Charge (RAC) in Mazatlán, Mexico.

Mazatlán is one of the most beautiful cities in the world. Lush and gorgeous on the shoreline of the Pacific, it is sandy beaches, big-big game fishing and honeymoons. Hell, it's where the *Love Boat* used to dock on every episode of that show back in the 1970s. With my new position as RAC, the administration rented us a place that looked like it could have been on a postcard. It was a five thousand square foot mansion on the water with an Olympic sized pool and full-time staff that included a chef, maid, chauffeur, a crew of gardeners and a zoologist. That's right, *a zoologist.* An eccentric and wealthy doctor owned the house and he filled it with wildlife that lived on the grounds. The place came with iguanas the size of small cats. A family of raccoon-like animals called cacomistles. And a mischievous spider monkey named Charlie who I would eventually try to kill. It was like I was finally living the life I had *pretended to be living while undercover.* My wife and little girl could not have been happier. But as nice as Mazatlán was, there was a reason the DEA supplied us with 24 hour armed security personnel. It was as dangerous as it was beautiful. Because Mazatlán was in the Mexican state of Sinaloa.

As a general construct, it is almost indisputable that certain geographical areas at certain times often foster and create a specific type of vocation. 16th century Florence produced some of the greatest artists who ever lived. Detroit in the 1960s gave us Smokey Robinson, Marvin Gaye and the Motown Sound. But consider that from the mid-1980s through the '90s there was, without doubt, no area in the world that manufactured more violent, reprehensible and atrocious drug lords than the state of Sinaloa, Mexico. Ernesto Fonseca Carrillo was from Santiago de los Caballeros. Rafael Caro Quintero was from Badiraguato. Miguel Ángel Félix Gallardo was from Culiacán. El Chapo was from La Tuna. Ismael "El Mayo" Zambada García was from Badiraguato. And Juan José "El Azul" Esparragoza was from Mazatlán, where my new home was located. The Mexican state was literally the cradle of drug kingpins — and

The Last Narc

also ground zero for what was the biggest turf war in the history of the illegal drug trade. I was assigned right in the middle of it.

By now I had been a DEA agent for over ten years and I thought I was pretty hardened. I had been shot at. I had killed. I had been a border rat in Arizona and had gone UC with some of the toughest criminals you can imagine. But nothing, and I mean *nothing*, could have fully prepared me for what I would experience in Mexico. There had been moments in my previous assignments that all agents experience. There is a cliff between good and evil. Agents are sometimes asked to go right up to that edge, walk it, breathe it. I had always tried to go even further. As a UC I wanted to lean over that edge, float above it, defy its gravity. But in Mexico there was no such cliff. There was no gravity. As a narc in Mexico, you didn't lean over the edge of evil. *You lived in it.*

· · · · ·

One of my chief responsibilities as the DEA's Resident Agent in Charge in Mazatlán was to liaise with the local Mexican Federal Judicial Police (MFJP). But the word "liaison" in the parlance of DEA/MFJP is much more nuanced than its strictest definition. Mexico is and was a narco-state. To work with the MFJP one was, by proxy, working with the drug cartels. But if you fully understood the underlying premise of their world, as I did, you could begin to navigate your way within it. The fundamental premise is: *All of Mexico is corrupt.* It bears repeating: All of Mexico is corrupt. This does not mean that every citizen of the country of Mexico is a bad person. Most Mexicans are very good people. They just happen to live and work in a country that is absolutely corrupt. It also does not mean that every member of the MFJP is corrupt *all of the time.* While every *comandante* is bought and paid for, because the lifespan of their drug lord employer is often short-lived, loyalties can shift rather quickly. My job as RAC was to sift through these alliances, gather information and make alliances of my own. My first opportunity to begin building these alliances came not even a week into the assignment when I received a call from a local *comandante* while in my office. Strictly speaking, a *comandante* is the "commander" in a given military hierarchy. Not so in Mexico. In Mexico, the *comandante* is the HMFC — the *head mother-fucker in charge* — wherever that may be, local police, military, or in this case, the Federal Security Directorate (DFS).

"Hector," the *comandante* said. "I've heard good things about you. You have balls and you tell the truth. I believe that you and I can work together."

"Well, I don't know what you've heard about my balls," I said. "But I will always be honest with you and I would love to work together."

He laughed. "Excellent. We just arrested three drug traffickers who are trying to move a big load of marijuana. Why don't you meet me at the airport where we're holding them? We'll go up, I'll show you around and we'll do our interrogation in the air. Afterwards, we'll have a drink and smoke a cigar."

"Great. Sounds like fun to me."

Less than an hour later, we were in the air. I was sitting in the cabin of a twin-engine transport plane with three suspected traffickers and two armed soldiers. We were flying over the west coast of Sinaloa, heading toward the Pacific Ocean and the *comandante* was standing in front of us like a tour guide. "*To your right, if you look hard enough you will see Las Labradas, one of the oldest ruins in all of Mexico... And over there..."*

He went on and on about this place and that place and I was sitting there without a clue as to where this was going. *What happened to the interrogation?* It went like this for some time until we were about 30,000 feet in the air and well over the water. He then turned to the traffickers and his expression went cold. "As you can see, I have shown our new DEA agent many a thing. But what I have not shown him is where you keep the marijuana you were intending to move into the United States. *Where is it?"*

Silence. The traffickers just sat there like they'd heard nothing. Then, as casual as if putting out a cigarette, the *comandante* moved to the cargo door, lifted the hatch and opened it. A mighty gust of cool air burst into the cabin and swirled about us. The yawning of the propeller engines was nearly deafening. Finally, I thought, I knew where this was going. He was showing off a bit on my behalf. It was Mexican machismo shit. He was going to show the new guy from America what a badass he was. One of the poor traffickers would get scared and they would all begin to talk.

Not quite.

The *comandante* stepped toward the traffickers, stood dramatically and with a point of his finger, singled one of them out.

"Him," he said.

One of the soldiers hurried over, pulled the trafficker out of his seat, pushed him toward the door and tossed him off the plane right in front of me.

What. The. Fuck.

All oxygen was sucked from the cabin and I sat as stunned as the two remaining traffickers. "Now," said the *comandante*. "Who else wants to go swimming?"

Welcome to Mexico.

· · · · ·

People might think when a DEA agent is assigned to a foreign post that their arrest and search authority transfers with them, but nothing is further from reality. When out of the country, DEA agents are merely officials reporting to the presiding U.S. embassy or consulate. They neither carry nor possess official authority. Everything an agent advances, accomplishes, cajoles or manipulates is of his own accord. Sure, foreign counterparts respect your DEA badge, but it is by your own gray matter, devices and savvy that move cases forward.

While my official mission as RAC was clear, the unofficial mission was murky, ill-defined and complicated at best. I often had to recruit informants without my counterparts' knowledge. I had to do innumerable favors for the cops, military contacts and other government officials who I would later use to take my cases to the deepest and deadliest levels possible. I had to give face, dignity, honor and even an official endorsement to the DFS's questionable hijinks in order to further ingratiate myself to them, all so they could make my investigations happen. In other words, I had to do whatever I could *to get my fucking job done.*

Consequently, not all of my work as RAC in Mazatlán was dedicated to drug-related investigations. Such was the case when I received a late night call at home from Raul Montenegro, who was a colonel in the Mexican army in Culiacán.

"Hector," the colonel said. "I need your assistance on Highway 15. We just had a shootout with some traffickers."

"Is anyone hurt?" I asked. "And are there any others at large?"

"No. We killed all six of them. Just need you to write the report."

Hmm... I thought.

I grabbed everything I needed to write my report, including a camera so I could take pictures of the crime scene. I also called Joe Martinez who was one of my agents in Mazatlán and gave him the details so he could set up a road block.

· · · · ·

The crime scene was at an intersection off Highway 15, out in the middle of nowhere. Even with no traffic it took me about 45 minutes to get there. Joe had already arrived and set up a road block with a couple of other agents, but it really wasn't necessary. On one side of the road, Colonel Montenegro and his men were waiting about. There was nothing in their demeanor that suggested they had just survived an intense shootout with drug traffickers. On the other side of the road there was a car that was shot to shit and six bloody bodies laid out in front of it. I nodded to Joe as I crossed the police line, walked over to the bodies and immediately noticed a couple of things. First, none of the supposed traffickers were wearing any shoes or socks. Second, each of them had been killed with a headshot right in the middle of their eyes. You didn't need to be Sherlock Holmes to know this wasn't the result of a shootout. *This was an execution.* As I stood there wondering how I would write out my report, Colonel Montenegro appeared.

"Agent Berrellez, thank you for coming." He shook my hand warmly.

"So what happened here, Colonel?" I asked.

"Oh, we had to chase down these criminal traffickers. We cornered them here and they came out of their car firing weapons. We had to kill them, señor."

"Yeah, I noticed. And you got all of them in the head too. You must be pretty good shots."

"We are indeed, señor."

I scratched my head. "What happened to their shoes?"

He looked at me quizzically. "Shoes?"

"Yeah, why aren't they wearing any?"

The colonel gave me a knowing smile. He leaned in and said, "You know what happened here, señor."

I didn't. But I did know what he was saying. He wanted me to corroborate his story in a report to the Estado De Mayor and to his general.

"If you write this report as we ask, señor, the general will be very happy," he added.

I understood. And I did as he asked, writing up the report as Colonel Montenegro relayed to me. There really wasn't any sense in writing up a conflicting report. It would be my word against his and his men's. It also wouldn't have fostered any of the good will I was trying to build up. So I wrote up my own separate report which I sent via secret teletype to the DEA in Mexico City. This not only kept my superiors in the loop but it covered my back. Most importantly, it would give me a card to play later. Having both a colonel and general owe me a favor was something I could use to my advantage.

• • • • •

My first months as RAC in Mazatlán were dizzying. Between acting as chief liaison with the DFS, bi-lateral case/investigation development, training counterparts in counter-drug skills, intelligence gathering, US-domestic case/prosecution support and ambassador and staff support, I was home less than I was as an undercover. On the rare occasions I managed to free up an evening to spend with my wife and daughter, we could never go out. Gunfire was a nightly affair. I had initially told my wife that the noises we heard every night were fireworks from the nearby cruise ships. That ruse didn't last long. She put two and two together and though we never went out after dark, she never once complained about it.

Thankfully, we were living in a mansion with every amenity we could have asked for. In addition to our pool and tennis courts, we had a state-of-the-art entertainment center, complete with a big-screen TV hooked up to a satellite dish that allowed us to watch American shows. The embassy even arranged for us to get the latest movies on DVD. Our home also featured a massive common room that we converted into a magnificent playroom for my daughter Crystal. We filled it with a life-size play house, hundreds of toys and dolls, even pinball machines and arcade games. The whole place was a literal wonderland. Unfortunately for me, it became a living hell. The reason for this can be summed up in one word that even today when uttered, still sends chills of terror running down the back of my spine: Charlie. Or as I liked to call him, *Fucking Charlie.*

Fucking Charlie was our spider monkey. I know everyone thinks monkeys are cute and affectionate and loyal. They aren't. They're dirty, moody, smelly rodents. But Fucking Charlie was something altogether worse. I don't even think he was an animal. I think he was a demon of some kind whose sole purpose of creation was to torment me. Fucking Charlie spit at me whenever I walked past his cage. He seemed to be able to shit on command and would hurl his defecation all over the grounds of our home. Our yard came with a beautiful man-made pond that we filled with koi. Fucking Charlie killed them off one by one, a crime we had originally blamed on our dog until I witnessed him sneaking over to the water, reaching in with his filthy paw and pulling out one of the helpless fish. *He was evil.* Having developed the uncanny ability to free himself from his locked cage (a skill I took far too long to figure out he possessed), he would take food from our refrigerator, hide my shoes, crush my cigarettes or throw my clothes in the pool. He saved his most obnoxious and disgusting personality trait for when we threw parties.

Our home was often shared with neighbors, friends and work associates from the consulate. My wife loved entertaining with barbecues or movie nights. Well, Fucking Charlie would also join the party by jerking-off in his cage. We eventually covered it with a tarp during our parties, but you could still hear him going to work inside of it. It was both disgusting and embarrassing. I came to hate the creature with such a searing passion that at times it interfered with my work. I would often catch myself at the office, fantasizing about taking Fucking Charlie up in one of our DEA planes only to violently toss him out of the cabin in mid-flight, just as the *comandante* had done to that drug trafficker. I enjoyed imagining his shriek fade away as he plummeted to his death. And maybe if he was lucky enough to survive the fall, a school of sharks would find him and take turns tearing him apart.

Chapter 11

Cochi Loco and the Gipper

Aside from the nightly gunfire, the inherent danger of my job and the horror of living with a possessed spider monkey, we settled into a good life in Mazatlán. Though I tried to establish a balance between my work at the DEA and my home life, it became increasingly difficult. By accepting the position as RAC, I may have made the right move professionally, but the job was not conducive to my marriage or family. I wish I could blame the profession. Law enforcement in general is tough on marriages. But if I blamed "the job" I would be lying. *I loved what I did.* I loved going after bad guys. I loved investigating, gathering my agents, loading up — and hunting. What I loved more than anything was *being in charge.* I enjoyed spear-heading operations and working with my Mexican counterparts. I was also well aware that I was not just responsible for dozens of other agents' lives, I was also responsible for their wives and children. I embraced it. And I was not alone in my thinking.

Most of the agents I worked with were the same, absolutely committed to our job. The DEA came before everything. In many regards, this sentiment is one of the reasons that the DEA is arguably the premier law enforcement agency in the world. But it is also the reason for one of the many casualties in the War on Drugs.

I'm not referring to the abject violence, poverty, addiction, corruption and death that drugs bring. I'm referring to the spouses left at home alone, the children who grow up waiting for daddy or momma to watch one of their games, or the mother or father who just wants to know if their kid is okay.

• • • • •

Commitment, pride and determination are all part of what makes a good DEA agent. But to be a truly great one, I believed there was another component that was necessary: *Obsession.*

When investigating a particular crime or particular person, as an agent you had to commit every ounce of your thought, energy and will to the case. You had to live with it 24 hours a day. You had to retrace steps that you took dozens of times, reread interviews you've read hundreds, dissecting the dialogue, reconsidering its tone and inflection.

You have to analyze and restudy the case again and again and again — from every angle imaginable. You must find out everything you can about whoever is the focus of an investigation. Not just their bio. Not just their crimes. *But who they are. What their soul looks like.* Such was my obsession with the drug lord Miguel Ángel Félix Gallardo.

Gallardo was actually a policeman at one point in his life, joining the local force at 17 in his native state of Sinaloa. It didn't take him long to figure out there was more money on the other side of the law, so he quickly moved into drug-smuggling. He began his criminal career in 1971 and over the next 18 years, he built what was the greatest drug empire ever assembled. As an original *capo* of the Guadalajara Cartel, Gallardo proved to be a trailblazer in the drug world. Not only did he dominate the marijuana market, he was the first Mexican kingpin to grow opium — the raw ingredient for heroin — on Mexican soil. He also had the vision and statesmanship to partner up directly with Colombian kingpin Pablo Escobar to move cocaine. By the time I was assigned in Mazatlán, Gallardo had become the most wanted drug trafficker in the world, known as El Padrino, "The Godfather."

I wasn't just obsessed with Gallardo because of his ascension to the top of the drug world. *Gallardo was behind the abduction, torture and murder of Kiki Camarena.* Everybody knew it. But despite the ongoing investigation into that horrific crime, it had yet to be proven. I had focused on Gallardo from the moment I set foot in Mexico as RAC. And after nearly a year into my post, an opportunity finally arose where I could nab him.

For much of his rise to power during the 1980s, Gallardo used a vicious psychopath as his chief executioner. The *sicario's* name was Manuel Salcido Uzeta, also known as "Cochi Loco," the "crazy pig." In the summer of 1987, Cochi Loco murdered Lorenzo Gorostiza, the chief of police in Mazatlán. This was nothing out of the ordinary. Police chiefs in Mexico were always on somebody's hit-list. But Gorostiza was no ordinary police chief. He was also the best friend of the Mexican Army's top general in Mazatlán, Jesus Gutierrez Rebollo. If there is one thing unique to Mexican culture and its people, something that trumps drug-lord loyalties, political allegiances, even their faith, it is their passion for *revenge.* There was no doubt in my mind that General Rebollo would want to avenge his *compadre.* And I was right.

About a month after Gorostiza was gunned down, General Rebollo called me into his military garrison in Sinaloa for a meeting. We had never met before, but he said to me, "Hector, I asked you to see me today because I want tell you, man-to-man, I want Cochi Loco's head. I want to see him dead because he killed my friend. I want him and I want him bad."

"Okay. How can I help?" I asked.

"You have informants into Cochi Loco?"

I did.

"Okay. I'll give you whatever manpower you need. Let's take down that motherfucker."

• • • • •

The informant I had into Cochi Loco was a double agent, a Mexican army intelligence officer. He had infiltrated the Gallardo faction of the Guadalajara Cartel, gaining their trust by providing them with information about military anti-narcotics operations. I directed the informant to get a message to Cochi Loco, telling him he needed to meet with him as soon as possible because he'd learned about a major operation the military was about to undertake against Gallardo — and against Cochi Loco himself. My thinking was that we could set up a meeting with the three of them, the DEA could nab Gallardo and then we could give Cochi Loco to General Rebollo as a prize.

A couple of days later we received good news. Cochi Loco and Gallardo very much wanted to hear what my informant had to say. They agreed to a meeting, but there was no way they would meet with him in Sinaloa — they knew General Rebollo was in charge of the military there. Gallardo and Cochi Loco were under the protection of the Mexican general of Jalisco. They would only meet in Guadalajara.

This was a problem. I went back to the garrison to speak with General Rebollo a second time.

"General. I can set up a meeting but they won't do it in Sinaloa, only in Guadalajara."

What the general said next shocked me. "I don't give a fuck where we do it. I will take them down anywhere."

I was stunned. In Mexico's "cartel land," venturing into other territories without military protection was almost certain suicide. This also spoke volumes as to who the Mexican people really are. At their very core, honor trumped all.

"Are you serious?" I asked.

"Fuck yes. How many men do you need?"

"I need an army."

"You got it."

General Rebollo directed his number two, Colonel Horacio Montenegro, to handpick 100 soldiers from the 15th Military Unit in Culiacán, the capital city of Sinaloa. While he did that, I had my informant set up the meeting at Plaza de Sol, a famous shopping mall in Guadalajara, at a restaurant named Sanborn's. Together we worked out the logistics of sneaking our army from Jalisco into Guadalajara in the middle of the night. It was an incredibly dangerous plan on many levels — maybe even stupid. But that is one of the by-products of obsession. Sometimes training, diligence and common sense go out the window. I should have been worried about the whole idea, but I wasn't. I was something else: excited. I was about to bag Gallardo, the boss of bosses.

If I wasn't killed first.

· · · · ·

The informant wore a wire to the meeting. General Rebollo and I were able to listen, sitting among the 100 soldiers from the 15th Military Unit in troop trucks parked nearby. We all shared a nervous energy, but seconds after the informant walked into Sanborn's, it was clear that Cochi Loco and Gallardo weren't there.

"What the fuck? Where is Cochi Loco? Where is Gallardo?" we heard the informant ask.

A man's voice said, "Don't worry, don't worry. They want to meet you and they have a lot of money to give you for this information, but they didn't want to be seen in public."

I had heard that voice many times on wiretaps and immediately recognized it as Gallardo's uncle, a man known in the drug underworld as "El Cuchillo," meaning "the knife."

El Cuchillo continued. "Come, sit. Let's have a drink first and I'll take you right to them. They are waiting in a hacienda not far from here."

The general and I had to make a fast decision. We could wait and attempt to follow them in the hopes they would lead us to Cochi Loco. But this wouldn't have worked as we were in big, conspicuous vehicles. We could have also stormed the place and arrested El Cuchillo right then and there, but that would be a public spectacle. Cochi Loco and Gallardo would be warned long before we even began to interrogate El Cuchillo. I came up with a third option.

"I'm just going to go in and take the son of a bitch."

He looked at me like I was insane. "How are you going to do that?"

"I'm a DEA agent."

The general gave me a look that said, *so what?*

"I'll go in, bring him out quietly — you do the rest."

I tucked my .45 into my pants and started toward the mall.

· · · · ·

As soon as I walked into Sanborn's, I could see El Cuchillo and the informant sitting at a small table right in the middle of the floor. Without a word I moved toward them and sat down at their table. Obviously, the informant wasn't expecting to see me. His eyes got wide for a second. El Cuchillo was just as surprised as the informant. I waited long enough to make El Cuchillo uncomfortable before I said, *"Buenos dias, señor."*

He looked at the informant and asked, "Who the fuck is he?"

Before he could answer I jumped in. "I'm a fuckin' federal agent, motherfucker, and you're under arrest." I scooted my chair close to him and jabbed the barrel of my gun into his ribs.

El Cuchillo didn't bat an eye. "No, no, no. Wait a minute now," he said, as if there was a very simple misunderstanding. "My nephew and I, we're paying for protection. You can't arrest me. And you're going to get into trouble, my friend, because we're paid up all the way to Los Pinos." (Los Pinos is the Mexican White House.)

"Oh, really?" I said. "Did you pay me, motherfucker? Have you given me money?" I jabbed him even harder with my gun.

El Cuchillo may have been nicknamed "the knife" but no matter how tough a guy thinks he is, they all go soft when they know they're not protected — especially with a .45 digging into their ribs. El Cuchillo was no different. He deflated right in front of me.

"Okay, here's what's going to happen," I said. "You don't make a peep and we walk out of here right now or I swear to God I'll fuckin' kill you and ruin lunch for all these people. I don't give a fuck."

"What kind of federal agent are you?" he asked.

"The pissed off kind."

We got up from the table and I escorted him out with my gun firmly planted into his side. As soon as we were outside, the general was waiting with a small cadre of military guys in uniforms. I handed El Cuchillo over, they handcuffed him and quietly whisked him away into one of the nearby jeeps.

· · · · ·

We drove into a rural part of the country and pulled up alongside a road where thousands of acres of sugarcane was being grown. As soon as we parked, at the general's orders, El Cuchillo was yanked from his jeep and dragged into the sugarcane with soldiers close behind. I stayed back with a few other DEA guys I recruited. I had been in this kind of situation before, where the Mexican authorities used interrogation techniques that were a little "more aggressive" than what might be legal in the U.S. We hung back on the edge of the field smoking cigarettes, talking about the investigation. I figured the general was just going to smack the guy around until he gave up Gallardo's location, then we'd let him go. That's usually how it went down. But all of a sudden — *BOOM!* A gunshot. A moment later, the General and his men came out of the field. *With no El Cuchillo.*

The general proceeded directly toward his men. There was excitement in the air as they all checked their weapons, mounted up. I approached the general while he consulted with his colonel.

"Excuse me, General. I assume the informant gave up their location?"

"Sí," he said, without even turning to face me.

I asked the question I already knew the answer to.

"Where is the informant now?"

The general fell silent. He turned to me, reached into his pocket and lobbed me a Presidential Gold Series Rolex with diamonds all around its face. It had to be worth at least $50,000.

"He wanted you to have it. He won't be needing it anymore," he said with a grin. He and the colonel chuckled — and I got pissed.

"We're after Gallardo and Cochi Loco," I said. "We didn't come for El Cuchillo." And I chucked the watch back at him.

General Rebollo glared at me. We were working together and I had disrespected him in front of his men. It was a breach of protocol. He straightened, walked toward me and stood inches from my face. "And thanks to El Cuchillo, we can still get them. You are no longer in Los Angeles, agent. You are in Mexico. And we do things the Mexican way."

He turned and walked away.

· · · · ·

I was usually never nervous before a big raid, but as we drove to the destination, I grew uncertain about this one. I thought I had been using General Rebollo to get to Gallardo. I sat in the backseat thinking maybe it was Rebollo using me to get to Cochi Loco. It didn't help my mood that the general kept looking back at me. He had held on to Cochi Loco's watch and waved it at me playfully, repeating, "He won't be needing it." Every time he said it everyone laughed, as if it were the funniest joke ever.

The location El Cuchillo gave up was a small hacienda, isolated and sure to be heavily guarded. Even with over 100 men and the element of surprise on our side, there would be blood — and potentially a lot of it. As we headed toward the hacienda, all of a sudden there was a military roadblock ahead. We pulled over. Parked. Got out. It was a group of about 30 soldiers and they were with their general — Vinicio Santoyo Feria, who must have found out about the operation. I approached with General Rebollo and his colonel. General Feria stepped forward. He looked like Fidel Castro, short and stocky, chomping on the nub of a small cigar.

"What the fuck are you doing in my territory? You are out of your jurisdiction," he snapped.

General Rebollo told him that he and his soldiers from Culiacán were conducting a joint operation with the DEA. He introduced me as the DEA agent in charge of Mazatlán. I offered my hand but he rebuffed me.

"You have no idea what you're doing," he said to me. "You should get the fuck out of Guadalajara before I have you killed."

Everyone looked at me for a response. I had already disrespected the general I was working with. I figured, *why not another?* So I told him, "You know what, general? You're a crooked motherfucker and everybody knows it, so why don't you just go fuck yourself and pray I don't arrest you too."

General Feria was furious. He yanked the cigar from his mouth and threw it down like he was ready to fight. He glared at all of us, disgusted, before barking out an order to his men that had all of them falling back.

I knew what he was doing. He was doing his job. If he knew that we were on our way to raid a hacienda where Gallardo and Cochi Loco were holed up, then it was sure as hell that Gallardo and Cochi Loco knew this too. By stopping us with his little show of strength, he was giving his boss some extra time to clear out. And it worked.

Less than an hour later, we raided the hacienda. There was mild resistance and we ended up shooting a few bad guys. We seized several kilos of dope and the information the military obtained from the cartel gunmen we captured led to several more huge busts over the next few days. But the general didn't get Cochi Loco. And more importantly, I didn't get Gallardo.

• • • • •

About two weeks later, General Rebollo called to invite me to a celebration of all the arrests and dope seizures. The party was hosted at the 15th Military Zone Garrison in Culiacán. All the soldiers who had participated in the operation were there as well as a bunch of colonels and lieutenant colonels, plus. While neither the general nor I had gotten our man, our alliance had proven to be a "successful failure." And that was good enough for everyone. We celebrated deep into the night, smoking cigars, drinking tequila and sharing stories. When the party was finally coming to an end, the general made a closing toast congratulating all of his soldiers and praising them for their courage and loyalty. Then he turned his glass to me and said, "And Hector, as a token of our appreciation for the invaluable assistance provided by you and the DEA, I have bought you this gift."

He handed me a small box. I opened it. Inside was El Cuchillo's Rolex. The whole room held their breath, waiting to see how I would respond. I had to go along with the joke. This time I beat him to the punch, saying, "He won't be needing it!"

We all laughed like hell.

• • • • •

There was one time in my job as RAC when suddenly, everything came to a halt. All briefings were postponed. All cases put on hold. All calls rescheduled. It was February of 1988 and it came when the United States announced that President Ronald Reagan would be meeting Mexican President Miguel de la Madrid in Mexico.

American-Mexican relations had been fraying for the better part of a decade. America blamed many of its cultural problems on Mexico, illegal immigration and the cost and crime that came with it. The influx of illegal drugs caused devastation in communities all over the country. Mexico, in turn, expressed resentment at this U.S. criticism. They countered that the country's porous border and cheap labor only encouraged illegal immigration, and that it was American's voracious consumption for drugs that was at the very root of the problem. Exacerbating any potential peace was the fact that Kiki's abduction, torture and murder still had not been solved. Both sides were frustrated and angry. But with the leaders of the two countries entering their last months in power, the two planned a summit that would be symbolic. It was a message to the world that the two countries were still bound to one another, not just by geography, but by common values and mutual goals. And this summit would be held *in Mazatlán, Sinaloa.*

As soon as the summit was announced, I was called in by both the FBI and Secret Service to lend my support and expertise. As far as I was concerned, they needed it. Mexico was the most dangerous country in the world. Sinaloa was the most dangerous state in Mexico. And Mazatlán was, most likely, the most dangerous city in Sinaloa. The powers that be on both sides could not have picked a worse place for a meeting between anybody — let alone two world leaders. To make matters worse, they chose the Camino Real Resort as the meeting place. Located on the beach of one of the world's most stunning shorelines, the resort was sure to offer some beautiful photo ops, but it was a logistical nightmare for police and Secret Service. The resort was open — no barriers. It was elevated, creating a clear line of site from a myriad of angles. Not only was the resort accessible by land and water, there was only one single road that led to the resort's entrance/exit.

It's often rumored that inter-departmental agencies sometimes have difficulty working together. There is an inherent, healthy rivalry between them, but there is also pride and ego involved. I had run into it throughout my career. But when things go well and everyone does their jobs, nobody does it better than the Americans. I have to also credit the Mexican government and police for their professionalism and excellence. One of the saddest and most ironic state of affairs in Mexico is that there are *so many good lawmen and women.* It wasn't until I worked with them during the summit that I truly saw this. They too are outstanding at their jobs.

In less than ten days, a resort located in an area that had literally been at ground zero for the drug wars in Mexico was made safer than Disneyland. *At least for a few days.* When the summit arrived, every member on both sides who made this possible stood and walked with a little more pride. I was working in the lobby of the hotel, feeling just that when I was tapped on the shoulder by a Secret Service agent.

"Agent Berrellez. He wants to meet you."

"Who?" I asked.

"The president."

"The president of what?"

"The president of the United States."

· · · · ·

I was escorted to a suite on the hotel's top floor and ushered into a room where a pair of Marines stood guard. I was nervous as hell. *Why did the president want to meet me? Had I done something wrong?* A dozen scenarios raced through my mind, all of which ended with me embarrassing myself.

The suite was a hotbed of activity. There had to be at least a couple dozen people working feverishly. Men and women were reading on computers, others were huddled about in private conversation, reports were being written, phone calls being taken. Everyone was impossibly good looking. The men wore tailored suits. The women wore designer dresses. Hell, they could have had their own calendar. But I quickly realized that all these players were mere satellites that existed in the gravity of the man standing in the center of the suite where I was led. He was tall. Strongly built. Handsome. And when he smiled, it was like looking at a set of piano keys.

"Mr. President. This is Agent Berrellez of the DEA." President Ronald Reagan extended his hand.

"Agent Berrellez, good to meet you," he said.

I shook his hand but stood momentarily stunned. At my very core, I was still just a poor Mexican kid from South Tucson. Yet here I was, shaking the hand of the leader of the free world. *Oh, if my mother could see me now.*

"And it's an honor to meet you, Mr. President," I finally said.

"I just wanted to thank you for your service down here. And for your assistance in making this summit possible."

"It's my privilege, sir."

It was an absolute honor to be in front of the president, but I got the feeling this was the standard "meet and greet" he gave to any government employee he came across. Suddenly, an ease came over him and he seemed to drop his formality.

"Could I ask you a question, agent?" he said to me.

"Absolutely, sir."

"How corrupt is it down here?"

"100%, sir."

He gave me a double take. "*100%?*"

"Yes, sir."

He considered this and asked, "Well, is it safe for me?"

"It is now, sir."

He laughed and patted me on the shoulder. "Well, thank God for that!"

We shook hands again and I was escorted out.

I can't tell you what happened at the summit that day, though I know it went smoothly and without incident. But I can tell you that I probably wouldn't have known if a bomb went off or a group of terrorists kidnapped both Reagan and de la Madrid. Because I was in another dimension the rest of the day. And I couldn't wait to get home and tell my wife.

• • • • •

Like a hero, I burst through the doors of my home eager to share the exciting news. My mood dampened when I heard crying in the kitchen, where I found my wife hovered over our little girl, Crystal. I rushed to her.

"What's the matter, baby?"

"Charlie slapped me and took my ice cream," she said.

I looked at my wife who nodded helplessly.

Fucking Charlie.

I stormed out to the back yard where Charlie usually was. And sure as shit, he was sitting in front of his cage eating my daughter's ice cream. He saw me and immediately sensed danger. I charged. I wanted to kill the motherfucker with my bare hands. But he jumped up and tore off toward the nearest banana tree, scurrying up in a matter of seconds.

When I reached the tree, I looked up to find him safely hiding on one of the branches. He gave one of the smuggest looks I've ever seen. There happened to be a rake at my feet. I reached down, grabbed it and threw it as hard as I could at the little monster. Fucking Charlie dove out of the tree toward the wall, but along the way he clipped one of the electric wires that powered our house. It triggered a massive spark and Fucking Charlie shrieked in pain before he plummeted to the ground.

    Tentatively, I approached his lifeless body. All the hair on his body stood on end. There was even a small plume of smoke rising off his head. I had done it. I had killed Fucking Charlie. A burst of euphoria began coursing through my veins. But just as my joy came to a crescendo, like a slasher-movie villain, Fucking Charlie hopped up and ran off.

    I can't say that I was mad or disappointed. I was still in the clouds. I had just shaken hands with the president of the United States.

    Not even Fucking Charlie could ruin that.

Chapter 12

Los tallos sangrientos
The Bloody Stalks

The ritual was what I loved. The way she made the presentation. The rosaries around her neck. The crucifixes hanging on the walls. The mural of Our Lady of Guadalupe. And the lit *valadoras* that featured the Sacred Heart of Jesus, Saint Jude, Saint Michael. There were the cards too. But what I loved most of all was that it was just *mi mamá y yo*. Mom and I. As my life and career began to take bloom, I could only rarely speak with her on the phone, seeing her even less. Of all the things in my life that I had to sacrifice to the job, this was perhaps the toughest. It pained me to be away from my wife. It tortured me to miss my children growing up. But at the end of the day, I was *a momma's boy*. I was the one growing in her womb when she learned what was ahead for me during her time with the gypsies back in Nogales, Sonora.

My mother was sullen at the moment and this concerned me. I had sat before her my whole life, watching her read the cards. Even when the reading had been an ominous one, she had always delivered it with a hopeful glimmer in her eye. She had always read for me as if not predicting the future, but dispensing advice. This night was different. *This reading was different.* My mom studied the cards. She took in a deep breath and exhaled.

"Bullets are coming for you, my son," she began. *"I see the dead bodies of violent men. And I see blood running down the stalks of corn. But..."*

She hesitated, then closed her eyes for a long moment as I sat there helplessly, like I had when I was a boy, waiting for the last part of a story before being tucked into bed. *But what, momma?*

She opened her eyes, looked at me and finished. *"But you will live,"* she said.

It was the spring of 1988.

· · · · ·

By this time I had been promoted again, becoming the lead investigator of the DEA's international field office in Mazatlán. One day I received a phone call from a fellow DEA agent in Colombia named Tony Huerta. Huerta told me a reliable informant had provided solid information that a ship containing 20 tons of Colombian marijuana and one ton of pure cocaine had left Colombia and was headed for Sinaloa. The informant didn't know what city the ship was headed for, but he had given Huerta a phone number that supposedly belonged to the man who would be receiving this massive load of drugs.

I reached out to a source of mine at Telmex, the Mexican national phone company, who ran the number. It was registered in the name of Pablo Jacobo. The address on record was a tiny market in Navolato, a small city not far from Culiacán, the capital of the state of Sinaloa. Navolato is located near the coast on the Gulf of California, so it was in line with the information about the marijuana and cocaine arriving by ship. Plus, the place was a real shithole.

Even today Navolato is one of the most dangerous places in the world. Back then, it may have been worse: a hotbed of criminals and drug trafficking.

I looked into all the players in the Navolato drug game and found out very quickly that the federal police *comandante* in that region was on the payroll of the drug cartels. For that reason, I couldn't notify local cops. Instead, I called a friend of mine named Guillermo Gonzales Calderoni who was the deputy director of the Mexican Federal Judicial Police. I liked and trusted Calderoni and asked for his help. Calderoni obliged, but he could spare only 12 men. I only had eight. That was a little light for what was potentially a big bust. But I went with my instinct and we decided on a joint DEA/MFJP raid.

The next morning I was relieved to meet MFJP supervisor Jorge Rivera, one of Calderoni's best, most trusted agents. Jorge Rivera was a grade A badass and trusted ally. He brought with him a dozen of the toughest-looking Mexican *federales* I'd ever seen. Each one was strapped to the max and ready for action. Along with the two Humvees, eight men and 10,000 rounds of American muscle I already had, we were suddenly looking pretty formidable.

I gathered the joint team and debriefed them on all the information we had. Then I announced the plan: "Since we don't know for sure if the load has arrived or not, I want to go jack up this guy Pablo. If the load's still on its way, we'll get him to give up the time and place and take it down at the beach. If the load is already in Sinaloa, we'll make Pablo tell us where — and then we'll raid the motherfucker."

The team got fired up. This is what they were trained for. They were young guys, carrying high artillery rifles and wearing body armor in the sweltering heat of Sinaloa. They sure as hell didn't want to hear "stakeout."

Our joint unit headed to where the store was in Navolato, which was like driving to the middle of *the middle of nowhere*. Nothing but winding dirt roads and jungle. I didn't want the group to be too conspicuous, so we broke up our caravan. Jorge and I went in one of the trucks with a couple of agents. A couple of others were close behind. The rest of them followed until they were on the outskirts of the town, where they would stop and wait until I gave further orders.

The market wasn't exactly a 7-Eleven. It was more like a shack on an unpaved lot with a pair of skinny pumps out front. Not a soul in sight. After we parked, a half-dozen commandos and I, armed to the teeth, walked in. It was like stepping into a time machine — just an open floor with a smattering of shelves, semi-filled with cigarettes, candy, snacks. The walls had vintage advertisements for Coca-Cola, Gillette and Noche Buena. Behind the dusty little counter, next to the two-band transistor radio that was playing *norteño*, was one small Mexican man who looked scared shitless.

I led the men to the counter and squared up the panic-stricken cashier. Like most of the Mexicans I would come across, my first impression of the guy was one of empathy. With his ill-fitting Levi's and knockoff fútbol jersey, the guy looked poor. His pockmarked face suggested a long and losing battle with acne during adolescence. But I could never show softness. Ever. Because giving off just a whiff could get me killed. Still, I took comfort in knowing that I was still capable of feeling. *I could still be human.*

The Last Narc

One thing I had learned over the years while working in Mexico was that even though I was fluent in Spanish, I would speak and more importantly *act American.* You kick down a door and start barking en Español, the real *banditos* don't flinch. Or even worse, they open fire. But you come in Yankee-hard *and start giving orders in English?* You have their attention. Looking pissed, I turned to Rivera.

"Tell him we're looking for Pablo."

Estamos buscando Pablo.

"Pablo no está aquí," said the cashier.

Eyes volleyed back to me. I reached over and turned off the radio. Letting silence fill the room, I kept the coldest glare I could muster on him.

"Where is he?" I finally asked.

The question needed no interpretation. Nor did his answer.

No lo sé.

The cashier then began rambling desperately, pleading innocence. Rivera tried to keep pace. Something about *him not having anything to do with anything...That he's just a worker, blah, blah, blah.* I put an end to it.

"ENOUGH. What the fuck do you mean?!" I barked. "Pablo owns this fucking place. So either you're Pablo, or you work for him. Cut the bullshit."

The cashier held his stance. *No lo sé... No lo sé...* But while he did, I noticed him slowly reaching for the handle of a drawer in front of him. Without hesitation, I lifted my AK-47 and stuck its barrel right on his forehead. For the first time, *I spoke en Español.*

"Freeze, motherfucker, or I'm going to blow your head off like it's a watermelon."

Oh, he froze alright. He might have fainted had Rivera not reached over and grabbed him. Then I played my best card. It was a bluff.

"I'm going to ask you one more time. *Where is the drug load, Pablo?*"

And just like that, the fearful little cashier changed his disposition. He straightened, shedding his cowardly ruse completely. He looked me square in the eyes and said, "It's at my ranch in Limoncito."

I almost wanted to applaud the guy's acting chops. Dude was better than Pacino.

"Is anybody there?" I asked.

"No, just my ranch hands," Pablo said.

"Are they armed?"

"No, they are not."

"You're telling me you've got 20 tons of marijuana and one ton of coke, and there's nobody guarding it but some peaceful ranch hands who have no guns?"

"Yes. That is what I'm telling you."

I thought long and hard then looked at my men before turning back to Pablo.

"Okay, well, let me tell you something. You're going to lead us to your ranch, and when we get there I'm going to put you on the front of my car like a fucking hood ornament. And if anybody shoots at me, they're going to hit you. So you better not be lying to me, motherfucker. Do you understand?"

"I'm not lying. There will be no problems."

· · · · ·

The Last Narc

Limoncito was a little town about 20 kilometers from Navolato. The name comes from the Aztec for "little lemon." It was one of the richer agricultural areas of Sinaloa and one of the more beautiful. Located in the valley of the Sierra Madre Occidental and the Gulf of California, it is a colorful landscape of jungle and farmland. My caravan and I made the long drive, cutting down dirt roads that went through miles and miles of sugarcane, rice and wheat fields. All the while, Pablo Jacobo said not a word. He just sat there, cuffed, staring straight ahead. After what seemed much farther than what we'd travelled, Pablo asked me to stop the convoy. He nodded to a single, narrow dirt road leading off the main one. In the distance, about a half kilometer away beyond the trees, I could see a ranch.

Pablo assured me that the dirt road was the only way for a vehicle to get on or off the property, but I still sent a couple of men to scout around. About 20 minutes later they returned and confirmed. *Nada.*

Though it seemed like it would be a routine raid, something wasn't sitting right with me. While the scouts did their reconnaissance, I studied the ranch at a distance with my binoculars and didn't see a thing. But that's what rubbed me. *I saw nothing. Nobody.* I pulled Rivera aside.

"If this motherfucker is lying, we could be walking into an ambush."

Rivera agreed. "Maybe we should call the police?"

We smiled, then thought for a long moment.

"It's your call, Hector," Rivera said.

It was.

"Okay," I said. "Duty calls. We gotta take it down."

The group loaded back onto their vehicles and we started down the narrow dirt path. I drove the lead vehicle with Pablo sitting right beside me. In the vehicles behind me there were eight DEA tac guys with M-16s, fully automatic, and a dozen MFJP guys who held AK-47s, also fully automatic. We had over 10,000 rounds of ammunition.

I took it nice and slow.

About 400 yards from the ranch, the dirt road was heavily shaded by large banyan trees with kidneywood in between. It grew so thick that under the oppressive Mexican sun only shards of light survived. It gave our path an eerie, foreboding appearance. Each man on the convoy clutched his gun. I could feel it.

I thought of my men. I always did before a raid. *They were my responsibility.* I knew they were each professionals who prepared in their own way. Some, like me, from the divine. Some from the Copenhagen between gum and lip. And some were just born for it. But no matter how they prepared, I knew this was the moment that bound us. This was the moment they too would learn to feel. Because this was the moment mystery mastered fear.

At 300 yards, there was still nothing moving up ahead at the ranch. Even the animals were quiet. We got to within 200 yards. Then 100 yards. Then 50. As we came into a clearing that opened into ranch's main property, a peaceful calm began to wash over me. I thought *maybe Pablo was telling the truth.* But it only lasted a moment. As soon I stopped and parked I turned to Pablo, who had a strange look about him. I had seen that look before and I could read it. *The man had a secret.*

"Pablo, how many men are here?" I asked.

I will never forget the expression on his face as he turned to me. It was painted in the unholiest of smiles. I looked around and was suddenly seized with an awful realization.
We were in the middle of a cornfield.

• • • • •

I didn't hear the gunfire but a deafening thunderclap that coincided with the front of my windshield exploding. What followed was a hurricane of bullets that seemed to be coming from everywhere. Instinctually, I flung open the door and dove for the ground.

When I was a boy, there was a saying my father used when teaching me how to box. He would say, *"All tactics go out the window when you get hit."* What he meant was that no matter how well-conditioned I was, no matter how well-prepared I could be, all of my training and tactics would go out the window the moment I got punched. This is what I was thinking as I was on the ground crawling beneath the hellfire. I hadn't just gotten hit. I had gotten hit with a sledgehammer.

And it didn't stop.

The crack of gunfire was coming in stereo, a staccato of percussive, concussive blasts that sent fragments of dirt, glass and gravel flying into my body like shrapnel.

I continued crawling. I could hear the bullets as they ripped through metal and caromed off stone. I could also hear the cries of some of my men as they were hit. I turned back to get a glance at the damage and was horror-struck to see one whose arm had been nearly completely severed at the shoulder, blood jetting from it like a spigot. On the ground not far from him, another *federale* was splayed out, lifeless. Their truck was being ravaged by bullets and bursting from its battery was a sprinkler of steaming acid. All of it, the carnage and the damage, the chunks of Earth that erupted out of the ground, seemed to defy gravity. Like a twisted version of a snow globe that had been shaken up, only this one wasn't an idealistic Christmas scene. *This one was hell.*

I moved fast on my belly until I reached cover by a reinforced concrete water trough. Once there, I quickly surveyed the battlefield. I could now see at least a dozen gunmen firing shots from every corner of the ranch. Though they made a lot of noise, none had a clear line of site to our position. *Somebody else was doing the damage.* I looked up and there on top of a grain silo was a gunman, just unloading. *Motherfucker.*

Our unit was pinned down. Several of my men had been shot and at least two were lying prone and motionless. I would later find out that it was far more than a dozen bad guys with guns. It was 19. And each was firing an automatic rifle. There was so much gunfire coming at us, we couldn't even think about shooting back. So I just stayed down, helpless, listening to the dark orchestra of bullets swirling about.

At some point during the initial onslaught, one of my agents, Sal Leyva, came crawling out of nowhere toward me. "What the fuck?!" he yelled over the noise. "We are going to die here!"

The thought had crossed my mind.

The agent stared at me. I was his superior. I had to do something but I was momentarily paralyzed. *What could I could do?* If I even lifted my head it would've been blown off. I continued to stay down. *Think*. And as I did, I remembered my mother's premonition: *Bullets are coming for you, my son, but…*

You will live.

I considered her words. I loved my mother. By most accounts, she was a gifted fortune teller. But let's face it, her prophecy wasn't exactly a science. *How could she be sure?* And yes, I might live through this shit, but what if I was shot through the spine and ended up paralyzed? Technically she would have been right, but it would hardly be any consolation if I spent the rest of my life in a wheelchair or shitting into a plastic bag. Given the situation, it was in my best interest to stay down.

Then something happened. I reconsidered her words and said to myself… *Fuck it.* No, I didn't get brave. Every DEA agent who put themselves in the line of fire was brave. Something else clicked inside me. Something that can sometimes be far more virtuous than bravery. *I got fucking crazy.*

I rose with my AK-47 over the top of the water trough and fired a burst of shots toward the ranch. Then I gave the command to my men. "SHOOT BACK!!"

And that's all it took.

All of the agents who'd been under cover followed my lead. They aimed their weapons and opened fire, unleashing a furious ardor of Mexican-American bullets that hit the ranch like a tsunami. And just as suddenly, it was the cartel's gunmen diving for cover.

I used the moment to step up and take aim at that bastard up in the silo. I unloaded. And unloaded. And unloaded. Three full magazines. 60 round clips. 180 bullets. The shots left the silo smoldering and obliterated. There would be no more bullets coming from above.

Our joint unit continued to shoot. We may have had less men, but we were the superior soldiers. With our mighty opening salvo, I could now see what my mother had seen: *The dead bodies of violent men. And the blood on the stalks of corn.* But the cartel would dig in and reengage. What ensued was a straight-up, back-and-forth gunfight.

And it lasted for over an hour.

As time went on, I became aware that all of our men who'd been shot were still alive. But some were lying there out in the open. They couldn't crawl to safety because of their injuries. They were bleeding out too. I knew we had to do something or they were going to die.

One of my agents, Jim White, was taking cover behind an SUV and miraculously, its engine was still running. I yelled out, "Okay, everybody! Jim's going to back up the truck to get close to our wounded guys! When I give the word, I need everyone who's not wounded to open up on those motherfuckers with everything you've got! We need covering fire!"

White was an incredible agent. Smart. Ballsy. Always listened to orders. But he turned to me and said, "What the fuck do you mean *I'm going to back up the truck*? They'll blow my head off the second I get in the driver's seat!"

"Then fucking stay down!" I yelled.

White did as he was told. He dove into the SUV's front seat, stayed down and dropped the truck into reverse. I jumped up from behind the water trough and snuck behind the SUV as it backed up. The cartel's gunmen saw the vehicle moving, figured something was up and turned their firepower on it. Bullets began showering on it until I gave the order to open up hard. Our joint force obliged.

It would give us all the time we needed. I grabbed one body. A couple of the MFJP guys broke from cover and grabbed the others. The wounded were literally flung into the back of the SUV.

I hopped in the passenger seat and White pulled a hellacious U-turn before flooring it. The vehicle roared down the dirt road back toward the paved highway and we turned same way we had come in. White kept the pedal down until we neared 100 mph. We were both so pumped with adrenaline it hadn't occurred to us that *we didn't know where the hell we were going.* So we kept driving. The men in back were moaning in pain, but they were alive. One of them with a gunshot wound in his chest asked for a cigarette. I gave him one and we watched as he inhaled and a small plume of smoke drifted out of his chest wound. We all cracked up. Agent humor.

Up until that point, we had seen no other vehicles on the road. But we spotted a car coming from the opposite direction. I had White pull over and stepped out to flag it down. As the car approached, I could see that it was both bright yellow and a piece of shit. It was a taxi cab. I had it slow to a stop before its driver climbed out, waving his hands hysterically.

"Please, señor, don't kill me!" he said. "Don't kill me!"

I had forgotten that I was covered in blood and, oh, also happened to have an AK-47 hanging off my shoulder.

"It's okay," I said in Spanish. "We're Mexican *federales!*"

The cab driver glanced over to Jim White, who looked like his name — blonde hair and blue eyes. He turned back to me with a vexed look. "What kind of *federale* is that guy?" he asked.

I didn't answer. Instead, I said, "I'm ordering you to get in the truck with my partner and guide him to the closest hospital. We've got injured men."

"What about my taxi?"

"I'm going to need to borrow it for a couple of hours."

"Señor, that taxi is my livelihood."

"Don't worry my friend," I assured him. "You will get your taxi back. I *promise* you."

I turned to White. "You call DEA headquarters in Mexico City as soon as you get to the hospital. Tell them we need reinforcements and we need them NOW."

I hustled toward the taxi.

"Where the fuck are you going?" White asked.

"Back to the shootout," I said. And I slipped behind the wheel of the taxi cab and took off.

· · · · ·

The gunfight between the DEA/MJFP and the cartel had settled into a rhythm. Shots would be sporadic for a time. Then intensify. Then climax, before receding again. They were just intensifying when, strangely, they slowed to a stop. Both sides of the battlefield turned their attention to the dirt drive where a piece-of-shit taxi was chugging its way into the arena. *What. The. Fuck.*

It was me. I pulled the yellow jalopy right up to the rear of the bullet-riddled DEA vehicles. It was surreal. Fearing I would be shot by my own men, I rolled down my window and yelled out, "Don't shoot me, motherfuckers! It's me, Hector!" They didn't. But the *pistoleros* sure as hell tried. They peppered the taxi with bullets, taking out its windshield, shredding its hood, but I rolled out and slipped into cover behind the cab before they could hit me.

The gunfight picked right up where it left off.

From that point forward, there were long breaks in the shooting, five, ten minutes, fifteen minutes. Both sides were getting low on ammunition. I must have smoked a dozen cigarettes while behind that taxi. About three hours after the ambush started, Jim White showed up with a platoon of Mexican Army soldiers. They had heavy machine guns, M-60s and stormed in like the cavalry. I asked the captain if they had hand grenades and he retrieved a box. I started launching them, but didn't have the arm to make it to the ranch. Thankfully, they had an M-79 grenade launcher and I was able to hit my target at will.

Our team arrested 15 of the gunmen, half of whom were badly wounded. Four were shot dead. On behalf of the MFJP, Jorge Rivera seized the 20 tons of marijuana and the ton of cocaine. It was such a large bust they had to call a semi-truck to pick up the load. I never saw the pock-faced cashier Pablo Jacobo again. I later heard that he was prosecuted and sent to prison in Mexico along with his gunmen.

All of my agents would live. Four MFJP agents wound up being air-lifted to a U.S. military hospital near San Diego. Some had been shot as many as seven times. The agent whose arm had nearly been taken off at the shoulder by AK-47 fire had to have it amputated, but otherwise, they all made full recoveries.

• • • • •

Two weeks after the shootout, I was in my office when my secretary poked her head in and said, "Mr. Berrellez, there's a taxi driver in the lobby who wants to talk to the agent who stole his taxi cab. Do you know what he's talking about?"

"Oh, shit…" I had totally forgotten about it. I got up, walked beyond the security door and into the lobby. And sitting there waiting was that poor cab driver.

"What's up, señor?" I said.

"I came to see you, señor, because you said you were going to give me my cab back, but you did not."

"Yeah, I kind of forgot about that. I'm sorry."

"Well, can I have it back?"

"Unfortunately, I don't think that's possible, my friend. It's been shot to pieces."

"It's been shot to pieces?"

I led the man back to the impound lot and let him see for himself. When the man saw his bullet-riddled car he let out a wail of despair.

"Señor, it's totally ruined! That cab was my life!"

I wanted to tell him that it was a piece of shit *before it was shot up*. But I truly felt sorry for the guy and wanted to make it right.

"Well," I started, "what was it worth? We'll buy it from you."

The dude's tears dried up real fast. "Seven thousand dollars."

"Seven thousand dollars?! Was there gold in the trunk or something?"

The man smiled. I knew that cab couldn't have been worth more than seven hundred bucks. But the fact was, it was the man's livelihood. And I had stolen it. And it was shot to shit. I wasn't going to start haggling over price. So I called Mexico City to speak with Country Attaché Ed Heath, who was in charge of the DEA in all of Mexico, and I told him the story. Heath had the same reaction I did.

"*Seven thousand dollars?!*"

"Come on, Ed," I said.

"Damn you, Berrellez," he said, wrestling with his conscience and his fiscal responsibility. Then, after a long moment, he approved it.

"Pay him," he said. And then he just hung up.

I went to the safe in the consulate and withdrew $7,000 in American cash. When I handed it to the cab driver, the guy looked like he had died and gone to heaven. Watching him walk away, I was struck with a deep feeling of gratitude. *I felt good.* About my job. And about my life. I had almost died just weeks ago. I had arrested bad guys. Saved good guys. And just when I needed some help, God sent me a taxi. *Life was good.*

It was about to change.

Chapter 13

Leyenda

"Hector, we need you to get out of Mexico, and we need you to do it NOW."

This was the DEA country attaché Ralph Saucedo calling, who had taken over the position from Ed Heath. It wasn't a request, it was an emergency order. Just weeks earlier, senior members of the Guadalajara Cartel had ordered a hit out on me. Initially, I hadn't thought much of it. Danger had been such a part of my life and work in Mexico that it didn't even register. However, these *sicarios* had gone one step beyond this threat. *They went after my family.*

Thankfully, I had prepared my wife for such a situation. And this is not an easy conversation to have with your spouse. Honey, just to let you know, *sicarios* may try to kill you and our children sometime while I'm at work. But I am glad that I did.

About two weeks after his order —while I was working a case in Jaripillo, my wife and five-year-old daughter Crystal were at the beach near our house in Mazatlán when a pair of strangers started to follow them. My wife noticed them, saw the way they were dressed and knew they were cartel gunmen. Reading their body language, she knew that she and our daughter were in serious danger. As the men got closer her intuition kicked in. She grabbed our daughter and took off running. The gunmen chased after them, but my wife was able to run to a neighbor's house before they could be grabbed. She immediately called me and I immediately called the DEA. Mexican soldiers and DEA agents stormed the beach house, whisked my wife and daughter to the airport and flew them directly to Tucson.

At first I stayed back in Mexico. I was so pissed, I wanted to keep working and find those motherfuckers. But the DEA would have none of it. I was too hot. They conducted an emergency evacuation, scooping me up and flying me to Tucson with nothing but the clothes on my back and the gun in my waistband. I left everything at my house in Mexico — all my furniture, my clothes, even my weapons.

For the next few months my life and my job were in limbo and I had nothing to do. I have to say, on paper I was living the life. I was boarded at the Marriott Hotel in Tucson, all expenses paid by the DEA. Every two weeks on payday the federal government transferred a nice little check into my bank account and I didn't have to do a damn thing. I spent time with my family without a worry in the world. You would think that I could have enjoyed it. No *sicarios* chasing after me. No gunfights. No guys getting tossed out of planes. And I hate to even write this, but I was miserable.

I was accustomed to constant action — an adrenaline junkie. I loved shaking down suspects, grilling informants, raiding drug dens. My job was a rush and suddenly I found myself with no cases to work, no assignments, no rush to be had. My biggest decision every day was, "Where should we eat dinner?" With each passing week, I became more and more agitated. Every time I called headquarters I got the same story: "Just stay where you are, Hector, someone will call you soon."

The Last Narc

Someone will call soon. My poor wife and kids. Here I was, the first time in my adult life that I had been around my family for an extended period of time, and all I could think of was when I would get back to work. I look back now at that time with great regret. In retrospect, it was probably the only time in my life when I was a good husband, a good father. Not because I didn't always take care of my family. I did. Not because I didn't love my family. I loved them more than anything. But for that brief period of time while I sat and waited for that phone to ring, I was present to them. I was a part of their everyday lives. I was a part of all the mundane, routine, ordinary and very rich drama that goes into a real marriage and family. And now that I am so far removed from that, as bad as I wanted to escape it, I would do anything to have another week or even another day of it. At the time, that call I waited for couldn't come fast enough.

· · · · ·

"Hector," the voice said. "Jack Lawn wants to talk to you. They want you in Washington right away." Jack Lawn was the administrator of the DEA. He was the big boss. This was the call I had been waiting for.

I hung up.

I was always getting calls from famous or important people. I would get messages from heads of state, celebrities, starlets. Somebody would always call and say they were Michael Jackson or Eddie Murphy or Julia Roberts. And it was always a prank. One of my dopey fellow agents trying to get a laugh. I would do the same thing on occasion. It's what agents did. Our job was very intense and we often clowned on each other to relieve the pressure. I had been receiving a great number of these calls while posted up, because everybody in the DEA's Tucson office knew I couldn't wait to get back to work. That made me an easy mark. But then the prankster called back.

"Hector, no bullshit," the voice on the receiver said. "Jack Lawn wants to talk to you."

He gave me what I was told was a "secure line." So I dialed the "secure line" and a woman's voice answered, "Administrator's office."

"Is this really Jack Lawn's office?" I asked.

"Yes, it is."

"Well, I don't know if this is a prank or not, but my name is Hector Berrellez —"

Before I could say another word, she said, "Oh yes, Agent Berrellez. He's been expecting your call. Please hold for the administrator."

I was thinking to myself, *Holy shit, is this really happening? Why would the administrator of the DEA want to talk to me? Did I do something wrong? Am I in trouble?*

The line went silent for a few seconds, then I heard DEA administrator Jack Lawn's voice. "Agent Berrellez," he said. "Good to finally talk to you."

"Thank you, sir," I said, not really knowing why the hell I was on the phone with him.

"I have a very special assignment for you," he said. "And I need a very aggressive agent, someone who knows Mexico and the drug traffic down there better than anyone. I want you to take over the Kiki Camarena murder case. I want you to lead the investigation.

I want you to bring his killers to justice. And I want you to do whatever it takes. How does that sound, agent?"

Like my mother's voice.

• • • • •

I almost wept tears of joy while Jack Lawn spoke to me. For me, the Camarena investigation was more than just an assignment. Not because it was a career-defining case, and it was. But more importantly, for what the case represented. Kiki was not only a colleague and friend, he had become something of a patron saint to the entire American lawman community. As an agent, he had personally brought havoc upon the Guadalajara Cartel, the founding fathers of the nascent Federation, and I was finally being tasked to find his killers. Administrator Lawn laid out the assignment. It would be a brand new task force and I would work out of the Los Angeles office where I would have the liberty to hand-pick any 20 agents I wanted.

"Do you have anyone in mind off the bat?" he asked.

"Yes. Give me about a half-dozen bright Anglo agents who are skilled in the legal aspects of putting together cases that will be slam dunks for the prosecution. They'll be my office guys."

"Okay. And your field operatives?"

"Pardon me for speaking frankly, but I need some real badasses to get this done. I need gunfighters, not bean counters."

"Be specific," he said.

"Give me Mexican guys with balls bigger than mine," I said. But I added "sir."

I thought I might have stepped over the line a bit. It probably wasn't good form to speak with the administrator so informally, but it got better when he asked, "What else?"

"I need a lot of informant money, sir."

"How much is a lot?"

"About $3 million, just for the first year."

Lawn hesitated a moment then said, "Done."

He went on to emphasize that the task force's sole objective was to do whatever it took to find and bring to justice those responsible for Kiki's murder.

"It's my privilege, sir." I said. "And I will do exactly that."

"Good. You're going to report to me, directly to me, and only to me, okay?"

"Yes, sir."

My head was spinning before I hung up. I couldn't wait to get started. I knew it would be a daunting assignment. I knew that really good agents had already tried and failed in what I was setting out to do. But I also knew that this was the case that would define me and my career. This was the case that would be the culmination of everything I had worked for. This was the case I was born for. Everything about the assignment seemed pre-ordained. And it even had the perfect name: Operation Leyenda. "Legend."

1960: My first badge in grade school – patrol boy with my brother Art

1962: Graduation photo from junior high – voted "Most Likely to Piss Off Two Governments"

1969: In the army, Fort Bliss, TX

1970: At the DMZ north of the 38th parallel in North Korea

1971: My first day on the South Tucson Police Force, with my father and brother Raul (Dad is holding niece)

1985: Mexican newspaper's account of Kiki's abduction and murder

1985: Quintero laughing with the press after being arrested for Kiki's murder

1987: Christmas with my daughter Crystal

2001: Speaking at the California Narcotics Officers' Association

2014: On my horse Bello

2020: Showing off Jasper at a parade in Palm Springs

PART THREE

CONFIRMATION

It is the secret of the world that all things subsist and do not die, but retire a little from sight and afterwards return again.

–Ralph Waldo Emerson

Chapter 14

Venganza
Vengeance

In the immediate wake of Kiki's murder, after the reality of what had been done settled, a wave of bloodguilt engulfed all who were involved in the crime. As the initial dread rippled through the most corrupt corridors of the Mexican government, leaders of the Guadalajara Cartel were struck with something else, something they were very unaccustomed to: *Panic.*

The murder of DEA agent Kiki Camarena by members of the Guadalajara Cartel was a nuclear missile into the hull of U.S. federal law enforcement. And just as cartel leaders and Mexican officials who were involved in the heinous act had feared, it also unleashed an American wrath that nearly eviscerated the entire Guadalajara drug trade and all those who took part in it.

Before Kiki's body was even found, so intense was U.S. rage that they shut down the border and hundreds of agents from the DEA, FBI and ATF all poured into Guadalajara. The U.S. military sent dozens of its most elite units. Doors were blown off their hinges from Jalisco to Mexico City. Informants were shaken down. Second tier drug houses were raided or even obliterated. And those *pistoleros* who so brazenly acted with impunity on behalf of their drug lord employers scattered throughout Guadalajara like cockroaches, fleeing for their lives.

So petrified were members of the Mexican government, they scrambled to give the U.S. some kind of narrative as to what exactly had happened. At first, they arrested a 22-year veteran of the DFS named Tomas Morlet Borquez and two of his men. They claimed to have reasonable evidence that he was the "mastermind" behind the crime. Americans knew it was a sham and Borquez was released almost immediately.

Meanwhile, the Guadalajara Cartel's kingpins were in a state of hysteria. Miguel Ángel Félix Gallardo fled the state. Rafael Caro Quintero fled the country. And Ernesto Fonseca Carrillo, Manuel "Cochi Loco" Salcido Uzeta and Juan José "El Azul" Esparragoza did the only thing they could do — *hide.*

American federal law enforcement's response to Kiki's murder is something that I am still proud of. American retribution to the act was unhesitating, furious and definitive. Less than six months after his death, the Guadalajara Cartel, the world's most powerful drug-trafficking organization, was torn apart. But there is one more enduring legacy to Kiki's death, one that is his greatest: *It would never happen again.*

Still, when I took over Operation Leyenda, the Camarena murder investigation was far from over. There were still holes in the timeline that needed to be solved. There were still questions that needed to be answered. Of the nearly 20 suspects that had been known to be involved in the crime, only a handful had been tried and convicted, and none of the major participants were under U.S. jurisdiction. But that was about to change. Four years earlier, all those involved in Camarena's kidnapping and murder had felt a grave panic in its wake. I wanted to instill a new feeling for those still at large: *Fear.*

Chapter 15

Los sospechosos
The Suspects

It was no secret that the primary suspects in the murder of Kiki Camarena were the kingpins of the original Guadalajara Cartel, the progenitors of the super-cartel that would become the Federation. These suspects included Ernesto Fonseca Carrillo, Rafael Caro Quintero, Miguel Ángel Félix Gallardo, Manuel "Cochi Loco" Salcido Uzeta and Juan Ramón Matta Ballesteros. There were at least another dozen known participants based upon forensic evidence that included Manuel Ibarra Herrera, the MFJP *comandante* who oversaw Kiki's interrogation, Rubén Zuno Arce, who owned the house at Lope de Vega, and Humberto Álvarez Macháin, the doctor who administered the injections of lidocaine into Kiki's heart to keep him alive during his torture. While the previous investigators had yielded an excellent and accurate idea of what happened at Lope de Vega during the fateful days of Kiki's torture, after nearly four years of assiduous work, U.S. law enforcement was still unable to build a case against any of the primary suspects or their accomplices. Not one of primary suspects who were involved in the heinous act had been brought to justice under American jurisdiction. U.S. prosecutors had only managed to indict and prosecute three minor co-conspirators. As a result, by

January 1989 when I took over Leyenda, the initial American fury that had been unleashed upon the government of Mexico and the Guadalajara Cartel had given way to a seething frustration for its lack of results.

Initially, one of the biggest obstacles that American officials faced in bringing the primary suspects to justice was the fact that the Mexican government was of little or no help. Their participation in the investigation following Kiki's murder was, at best, incompetent. At worst, it was flat-out obstructionist. In the wake of the crime, U.S. investigators were flooded with blowback, bogus ransom notes and fabricated leads from "anonymous sources." The most egregious of this misinformation involved an unwitting suspect named Manuel Bravo Cervantes. The MFJP had come up with an anonymous note claiming that Kiki had been held at Bravo's ranch near a village called La Angostura in the state of Michoacán. Bravo had been a former congressman of the state and was undoubtedly corrupt. But he had nothing to do with the Guadalajara Cartel and was not on the DEA's radar. Still, a joint raid with the MFJP was set. But when American agents showed up at MFJP headquarters at the designated time for the raid, they discovered that the MFJP, led by a *comandante* named Armando Pavón Reyes, had left two hours prior. The Americans jumped into their vehicles and sped off toward Bravo's ranch but when they arrived, they discovered a bloodbath. The MFJP had stormed the ranch, leaving Bravo, his wife and three sons all shot to death. (Bravo's youngest son, who had Down syndrome, had been shot while lying in bed.) There was no sign Kiki had ever been there. It was obvious that the Mexican government was attempting to throw American officials off the scent of those responsible. Why Bravo and his family were the sacrificial lambs would remain a mystery.

When not having to follow up hundreds of other dead ends, U.S. officials also had to deal with a flippant Mexican government attitude that bordered on indifference if not animus. An assistant to Mexican president de la Madrid once said to reporters, "How can the United States make such a scandal of this? You should not find it surprising that anybody fighting drug trafficking is abducted or killed." Not surprisingly, this sentiment was shared by most Mexicans. The Mexican people had learned to live in a narco-culture. You would have been hard pressed to find anyone in Guadalajara who was not a direct victim of the cartel's influence and violence. Unfortunately, there would be no unified rallying voice of change for one dead American. If anything, their unified statement was more akin to *welcome to our world.*

· · · · ·

It was only with unrelenting American pressure that the Mexican government moved on two of the primary suspects in Kiki's murder — Ernesto Fonseca Carrillo and Rafael Caro Quintero. On April 7, 1985, exactly two months to the day of Kiki's abduction, Fonseca's villa in Puerto Vallarta was surrounded by a joint operation of Mexican Judicial Police and *federales*. After a brief firefight with *pistoleros*, Fonseca called for a cease-fire and asked if he could speak with the commanding officer. He honestly believed he could simply buy his way out of the trouble he was in. It didn't work. He and all his *pistoleros* were arrested, tried and jailed without incident. However, Quintero's odyssey to justice was far more befitting a drug kingpin.

Immediately after Kiki's murder, he kidnapped a young girl he liked (who happened to be the daughter of a high-ranking Mexican official), hopped on a plane and bought his way into Costa Rica where he managed to continue his fabulous life as a drug lord. It didn't last long. The DEA tapped the home phone of the young girl he had abducted, anticipating she would eventually call home. She did. Less than a month later, the compound where he was hiding was stormed by an elite unit of Costa Rican police in conjunction with the DEA. He was then extradited to Mexico where he was tried and convicted.

While Quintero and Fonseca's imprisonment was meant to give the appearance of "justice served" to the rest of the world, those of us in the DEA viewed it as something much less. With no extradition to the U.S., the kingpins' sentencing wasn't punitive, *it was protective.* They were off the table for U.S. prosecution and every other major suspect as well as their co-conspirators were free. Gallardo was hiding openly in Guadalajara City. It was a running joke amongst agents at the DEA that everyone in Mexico knew where he was — *except for the police.* The same went for Rubén Zuno Arce, the drug lord who owned the house at Lope de Vega where Kiki was held, tortured and killed. Manuel Ibarra Herrera was not only still at large, he was still working as a *comandante* for the MFJP. Cochi Loco was still free. El Chapo, the man who moved Kiki to his final grave, was running loose and ascending. Juan Ramón Matta Ballesteros had finally been surrendered by Honduras and was being held in Mexico, but it was on charges unrelated to Kiki's murder. And the good doctor who worked hard to keep Kiki alive during his torture was going about his business as if nothing had ever happened. Just about every figure who had a hand in Kiki's murder was out on the streets and there wasn't a damn thing U.S. investigators could do about it. They simply could not develop a case against any of them. The reason was very simple: *They had no witnesses. Nobody would talk. And nobody could get them to talk.* All the witnesses who could testify against the primary conspirators were either too frightened to do so or so entrenched in the political hierarchy of the corrupt Mexican government that building a legitimate case without them was all but impossible. This fact was constantly underestimated by U.S. investigators. They simply did not get how corrupt it was, and still is, in Mexico.

    Here's the thing. *I did understand this.* I had worked on the border for years at the beginning of my career. I had ascended to Resident Agent in Charge of Mazatlán in my previous post. Unlike the prior investigators, I had a network of informants, *comandantes* and Mexican Judicial Policemen to consult, mine for intel and even leverage against. Most importantly, *I was Mexican.* I knew the people and understood its culture. I also understood something else: The U.S. had a secret weapon, a silver bullet for its war on drugs, especially in Mexico. It wasn't just our superior law enforcement agencies or the resolve of our agents. It wasn't our international statutes that allowed us to exert American justice globe-wide. And it wasn't our state-of-the-art technologies that have always been light years ahead of the rest of the world. It was and always will be the one thing that can cut through even the most maleficent corruption in the world: Money. We have it. We have a lot of it. And in Mexico, if you have enough money, *you can do anything.*

Before I started throwing around that money, I needed to throw around something else. *My weight.*

· · · · ·

Of the major suspects still at large, there was one who was particularly bothersome to me, and that was Rubén Zuno Arce who owned "the killing house" at Lope de Vega where Kiki was held and tortured. It was a known fact that Zuno was one of the most prolific drug producers in Guadalajara. He controlled massive marijuana and poppy cultivation sites in the mountainous areas near Mascota, Jalisco, Puerto Vallarta, Talpa de Allende, Tamasula and Apatzingan. As the brother-in-law of former Mexican President Luis Echeverria, Zuno was also one of the most well-connected and influential *narco-politicos* of the 1980s. He consistently and successfully interceded with Mexican cabinet and sub-cabinet politicians on behalf of the Guadalajara Cartel kingpins. According to numerous reliable and confidential DEA sources, it was Zuno who negotiated the approval for Fonseca and Quintero to cultivate the massive marijuana growing sites later discovered at Rancho Búfalo, Chihuahua.

Zuno was also a well-documented criminal in the files of Mexican law enforcement. In the 1970s, he was indicted on numerous counts of drug trafficking and other crimes, including statutory rape. In 1978, while two Mexican Federal Judicial Police agents were conducting surveillance of his residence attempting to serve arrests warrants on him, he approached them and shot them both in the face, killing them instantly. He fled to San Antonio, Texas where he remained in hiding for about five years — the time it took for his well-connected political family to nullify the criminal charges against him and arrange for his safe return.

Though Zuno had been investigated and cleared of any wrongdoing by the DEA's own station chief, it still chapped me that he was free. *Kiki had been killed in his house! He had to know something about what happened.* Zuno was still free when I took over Leyenda, having befriended Texas democratic congressman Albert Garza Bustamante, but he was also openly entering the United States. Passport records showed dozens of trips to the U.S. via the San Antonio International Airport. I wanted to put an end to this immediately and I wanted to talk to him, so I placed an outstanding warrant for his arrest as a material witness in Kiki's murder. I knew that Zuno was still protected and I knew that it might piss some people off, but I still had him flagged so that the next time he came into the U.S., I would be sure welcome him.

Within a month, Zuno made another trip to the U.S. via San Antonio and was placed under arrest by U.S. Customs and Immigration officials. I was giddy and began coordinating with U.S. Marshals for his transfer to L.A. But when Zuno's friend, Congressman Bustamante, learned that he had been placed under arrest, he went straight to the San Antonio airport and raised hell, screaming at the arresting officers and ordering Zuno's immediate release. I received a phone call from the supervising officer.

"Agent Berrellez. I've got a congressman here screaming at me to release this guy. I don't know what to do."

"You don't do anything," I said. "You keep Zuno there until the marshals come."

"But what do I do about this congressman?"

"Let me handle it," I said. And I hung up.

I reached out to Manny Medrano, who was both my friend and happened to be the Assistant United States Attorney. It was pretty late when I called him at home and I got a groggy, "Hello?"

"Manny, wake the fuck up. I need your authorization to arrest a U.S. congressman." "What...? Who? And what the fuck did he do?"

"It's Bustamante and he is obstructing justice by interfering in Zuno's arrest at the San Antonio airport."

I waited as he wrestled with his reply.

"Damn you, Hector. Going after congressmen now?"

"I just need you to have my back, Manny. In case he calls my bluff."

There was more silence, but I knew what his answer would be.

"Okay, Hector. I trust your judgment. If I have to file on a U.S. congressman, oh well."

Click.

I called the supervising officer back at the San Antonio airport and ordered him to put Bustamante on the phone with me. A moment later, the congressman was on the line.

"I am Alberto Garza Bustamante!" he barked. "I am a distinguished member of the United States Congress and I am demanding the immediate release of my friend Zuno!"

I told him in the calmest and clearest voice I could, "Mr. Congressman, Zuno is under investigation for murdering a U.S. DEA agent, and if by the end of the count of three you are still on this phone, I am going to personally drive to San Antonio and arrest you myself for obstruction of justice and interfering in a U.S. criminal investigation."

"You cannot do that!" he blustered.

I began counting, *one...two...* And the phone line went dead.

The customs official quickly called back to inform me the congressman had run out of their office.

"Good," I said. "Fuck'im." And I meant it.

The first arrest in any investigation may not be the most important, but it is oftentimes the most gratifying because it demonstrates a step forward. The arrest of Zuno may have pissed off people on both sides of the border but I didn't care. I wanted to fire a shot across the bow of the Mexican government, what was left of the Guadalajara Cartel and anyone else who would stand in the way of my quest for Kiki's killers. Herrera, Gallardo, Machaín, Cochi Loco, they were all in my crosshairs. I wanted to make it clear: Under my command, Operation Leyenda was going to move forward. But before I could go any further, I first needed *to go back.* Back to the beginning. Back to when Kiki was still alive. Back when the Guadalajara Cartel was the most powerful and dangerous drug organization in the world.

Chapter 16

Nido de los alacránes
The Scorpions' Nest

The Guadalajara Cartel was spawned of treachery and violence. During the 1960s and through most of the '70s, an organization known as the Pacific Cliqua dominated the drug trade in Mexico. At the time, drug organizations were not called "cartels," they were called *cliquas*, "clicks." The Pacific Cliqua was founded and had been run by Pedro Avilés Pérez, "El León de la Sierra," who was considered to be part of the first generation of major Mexican drug lords. A trailblazer in the smuggling of marijuana, Avilés was the first kingpin to use aircraft to bring drugs into the United States and smuggled cocaine through South America long before anyone had ever heard of Pablo Escobar.

Drug trafficking in the '60s and '70s was not the violent trade it is today. In fact, Avilés relied very little on violence to grow his empire. It was considered a threat to business. Instead, he utilized his organizational skills and business acumen, building Pacific's enterprise on Mexico's successful sowing, cultivation and distribution models. That would all soon change. Among Avilés' ranks were a trio of young, ambitious traffickers: Ernesto Fonseca Carrillo, Rafael Caro Quintero and rising *capo* Miguel Ángel Félix Gallardo. All would later claim that they learned everything they needed to know about drug trafficking while working in the Avilés organization. Perhaps they learned too much. It is widely believed that Avilés, who was killed in a shootout with the federal police in September of 1978, was set up by Gallardo who had risen to become the Pacific's treasurer. Gallardo, Fonseca and Quintero conveniently filled the void he left behind. Gallardo, who had spent time in Sinaloa working as a Sinaloan state police trooper and served as bodyguard to Leopoldo Sanchez Celis (the governor of Sinaloa), used his political connections to easily broker the protection of state officials. Fonseca used the organizational skills he learned from Avilés to set up their network and distribution. And Quintero grew their empire from the street, recruiting *pistoleros*, obtaining land and finding growers. The organization rounded out their hierarchy by pulling from the top of the former Pacific's ranks, including Fonseca's nephew, Amado Carrillo Fuentes and Juan José "El Azul" Esparragoza. Just beneath them were Cochi Loco, El Chapo, and Ismael "El Mayo" Zambada García. The majority of the organization's leaders were from Sinaloa, but they came to be known as the Guadalajara Cartel, named for their base of operations.

With their shrewd business sense, innovative distribution network and unique ability to not just understand the rocketing demand of the drug market, *but foresee it,* the Guadalajara Cartel exploded into the world's most powerful cartel. At their predecessor's best, the Pacific Cliqua had never supplied more than 5% of North America's voracious consumption of marijuana, less than 3% of its cocaine and only a fraction of its heroin. Within only two short years of its formation, the Guadalajara Cartel more than quadrupled those numbers. They invested massive resources into the growth, cultivation and distribution of marijuana. Their strategic alliance with the Medellín Cartel for the trans-shipment of cocaine proved to be brilliant. To exploit the incredible markup of opium into heroin, they even built their own refineries to mimic the success of the Golden Triangle's warlords. But their greatest business achievement was committing their largest expenditure to the one aspect of their business that could make them vulnerable: *lack of protection.* Ingeniously, if not diabolically, not only did they dole out enormous amounts of cash payments to ensure their protection from the local police, MFJP and all the way to Los Pinos, most of the cartel's hierarchy would actually be credentialed in the DFS.

By the spring of 1984, the Guadalajara Cartel had reached the height of its powers. While accurate figures of their revenue and profits can never be documented, most DEA officials placed the number well over $3 billion per year. To put this in perspective, had the Guadalajara Cartel been a Fortune 500 corporation for the fiscal year of 1984, it would have been one of the biggest corporations in the world, bringing in more profit than Mobil Oil, Ford Motor Company and Dupont — *combined.* The cartel did not just run Guadalajara, but through graft, bribery, elimination and intimidation, it ran all of Mexico with its influence pressing throughout Central America and up to the southern border of the United States.

·····

Throughout its meteoric ascent, the Guadalajara Cartel had always fashioned itself in the image of their leader, Ernesto Fonseca Carrillo. He was a notably conservative kingpin. Despite his enormous wealth, he did not live the lavish lifestyle of a stereotypical drug lord. He preferred to project himself more as a successful banker or lawyer. Though he dressed impeccably, wearing the finest suits imported from Italy with silk socks and hand-made shoes, there was nothing else ostentatious about his life. Parties at Fonseca's villa in Puerto Vallarta for cartel members and their families were notoriously staid. He exacted a rigid set of rules for his houseguests, restricting drug use, fornication or violence. It was Fonseca's outside rules that had built the cartel into the empire it was. He had a zero-tolerance policy on crime outside the spectrum of the cartel's primary business in the drug trade. Robbery, assault or homicide were all unacceptable and punishable by death. Cartel members were also not to interfere in the lives of ordinary Mexican citizens. But while Fonseca was busy acting as the cartel's business-like CEO, Guadalajara's youngest drug lord, Rafael Caro Quintero, would slowly begin to exert his influence in both public and, more importantly, inside the cartel's inner sanctum.

Quintero had always been the Guadalajara Cartel's wildcard. His ascension into the cartel's ranks began in his late teens and by the early 1980s, when he was still just in his 20s, he was worth about a billion dollars. He may have been uneducated and ruthless, but he also possessed an infectious personality. *He loved being a drug lord.* And those who surrounded him loved that he *acted like one.* Stories of his ostentatiousness are legend. He once showed up to buy a Learjet in Tucson and when the salesman told him the price, Quintero handed him a check and said, "I don't know how many zeroes that is. You fill it in." His signature nightclub departure after an evening of decadence was to throw tens of thousands of dollars in hundred dollar bills onto the dance floor and yell, "For you, my children!" The polar opposite of Fonseca's banker persona, Quintero dressed like a rock star, wearing the most expensive designer jeans and boots that could be made. Beneath his tailor-made shirts (which shouldn't have even come with the first four buttons since he wore them open-chested) were enough gold ropes to make Lil Wayne blush. He carried a $500,000 diamond-encrusted gun with his initials etched in rubies. If there was a woman Quintero wanted, he would simply take her. Literally. He would often kidnap underaged, pretty girls as young as 16 and bed them. In the event that their religiosity forbade it, he would travel with one of the many Catholic priests who were on his payroll. The priest would marry them on the spot and Quintero would proceed with deflowering them.

Fonseca and Gallardo always knew Quintero could be problematic. His antics had almost imploded the cartel shortly after its formation. As with most things related to Quintero, it was over a girl. In this case, a 17-year-old beauty named Sara Cosio who came from one of the most prominent political families in Guadalajara. As fate would have it, or at least the whim of a teenage girl, she fancied the dashing young cartel pilot Amado Carrillo Fuentes, Fonseca's nephew. Lines were drawn between the two men. Threats exchanged. Before the two would come to duel, Fonseca decided to transfer his nephew to a new location, sending him north to a border town in Chihuahua. The solution seemed to work. Both moved on and order was restored. While keeping Quintero close may have been Fonseca's greater intention, he surely underestimated the younger kingpin's toxic and larger-than-life persona. Fonseca and Gallardo may have been the Guadalajara Cartel's superiors, but there was no doubt that Quintero was its face. Much to their dismay, the Guadalajara Cartel would begin to take on his personality as well.

• • • • •

Despite the Guadalajara Cartel's staggering wealth and power, in the months leading up to Kiki's murder, there would be signs of its implosion. And it wasn't the result of pressure exerted by the DEA or the massive seizure of product at both Zacatecas and Rancho Búfalo. In fact, it may have been the opposite. The cartel had reached a point of what seemed to be invincibility. It was nearly impervious to product seizure. It was protected to the highest levels in the Mexican government. And the U.S., for all its bluster and the hassle of its pesky federal agents, was still its best customer. Quite simply, the Guadalajara Cartel had become too big, too wealthy and too powerful, all of which fostered a sense of hubris and invulnerability. Exacerbating all of this was the fact that key members of the cartel had broken what was the fundamental and most important rule of all drug kingpins. *They were using their product.* Fonseca, Gallardo and especially Quintero all enjoyed smoking their purest cocaine in the form of "bazookas," hand-rolled cigarettes sprinkled with cocaine. While its effects were not as dramatic as coke, it still delivered the same type of euphoria. They believed they could do anything. *And why wouldn't they?* Like rich, spoiled children, ranking members of the Guadalajara Cartel acted on any whim or impulse that struck them. *And they could get away with it.*

An example of this occurred at a party Fonseca held at his villa in Puerto Vallarta in the summer of 1984. Cartel parties were not Saturday afternoon barbecues. Though they weren't the bacchanalian fetes one may expect, they did come with massive consumption of alcohol, a smorgasbord of some of the best food in the world and would often last up to ten days. A couple of days into this particular fiesta, the drug lords decided they needed some entertainment — and they needed it *now*. Their solution was to hire internationally acclaimed singer Vicente "Chente" Fernández Gómez. Chente was known as "El Rey de la Música Ranchera," the king of *ranchera* music, and was like the Sinatra of Mexico. Needless to say, he was in the middle of a tour and unavailable. Not to be deterred, Fonseca dispatched some men to retrieve the singer while he was on stage in the middle of a show. Chente was then brought before Fonseca who happily greeted the singer and expressed, in advance, his gratitude for the singer's entertainment. Chente politely voiced his reservations, explaining his contractual obligations and his discomfort at singing before members of the cartel. Fonseca grew cold. "Listen to me," he said. "You are going to sing like a fucking bird. And you are going to sing until I tell you to stop."

Chente sang nonstop for three straight days.

While getting away with kidnapping a national superstar would certainly contribute to the cartel's feelings of both entitlement and impunity, they were also getting away with murder. *Literally.* 1984 would go on record as one of the bloodiest years ever in Guadalajara. And the violence was not exclusive to the cartel's drug trafficking business. Those who went on record against the cartel were killed, including journalist Manuel Buendía Tellezgirón, who wrote for one of the country's biggest papers, *Excélsior*. Even more telling than the cartel's mass murder of

Mexican citizens was their abduction, torture and murder *of Americans who were abroad.*

Less than two months before Kiki would be abducted, there had been at least six other verified abductions and killings of Americans undoubtedly carried out by members of the Guadalajara Cartel. On December 2, 1984, four Jehovah's Witnesses who had taken up residence in Guadalajara went knocking on doors in the city's upper middle-class Chapalita neighborhood, spreading word of their faith. The well-dressed missionaries, carrying pamphlets and books, vanished from the area that day never to be seen again. The four victims were Dennis Carlson, 32, and his wife Rose, 36, from Northern California, and Benjamin Mascarenas, 29, and his German-born wife, Pat, 27, of Ely, Nevada. Subsequent efforts by their families and Mexican police to locate them were to no avail. Less than two months later, on January 30, 1985, former Vietnam veteran John Walker and his friend Albert Radelat went to dinner at a Guadalajara restaurant when they too were abducted. But in this case, the two men would be found six months later — *dead.* Like Kiki, they too had been horribly tortured before being killed. Their bodies were buried in a shallow grave outside the San Isidro Mazatepec Park in Zapopan.

Despite lacking any evidence that these abductions and murders were related to Kiki's (which would take place only a week after Walker and Radelat's abduction), one needed to look no further than the fact that neither of the crimes had been solved. In Mexico, ordinary citizens didn't kill Americans. The reality that there had been zero arrests for any of these cases suggested with certainty that the perpetrators were associated with members of the Guadalajara Cartel.

At the very least, the heinous acts had clearly demonstrated a textured mix of paranoia, arrogance and violence that seemed to be pervasive in Guadalajara. Yet neither previous investigative teams had managed to connect the dots to Kiki's murder. It appeared to me that after Kiki had been killed, the DEA was so fueled with rage, so obsessed with avenging his death that they may have too aggressively poured their resources into finding out exactly what happened and who was responsible. Now that the smoke had cleared from that tragedy, as Leyenda's new chief investigator, I had an opportunity to do what the previous investigators were unable to: step back, study the entire case and analyze the complete picture. Only then can you begin to answer the first and most fundamental question of all murder investigations: *Why did it happen in the first place?*

Chapter 17

Engañados
Misled

Por favor, comandante! ... Por favor... No mas...
Please, comandante!... Please... No more...

This was Kiki's voice. DEA Administrator Jack Lawn had been given me copies of the tapes of his interrogation under torture when I had taken over the investigation. Though I wasn't there, I had to feel the last moments of his life as if I were in that room with him. I had to visualize and listen as he was beaten, burned, and sodomized — with malevolent satisfaction. I had witnessed many of these types of interrogations in Mexico while assigned the head of the DEA office in Mazatlán. They are beyond inhumane. They are savage. At one point, DFS agents had Kiki lying face down so one of the interrogators could jump off the bed and do cannonballs onto Kiki's body, landing with his knees into the middle of Kiki's back. I could hear the disturbing sound of cartilage ripping, bones cracking and the sizzle of skin burning. I wanted to know who each and every one of these executioners were, each and every beastly son of a bitch who was in that room.

Kiki's defeated voice faded in and out all through the entire sadistic soundtrack. It went on for hours. And hours. And hours.

It is one thing to hear a stranger cry out in pain and anguish, but it is another thing entirely when the voice behind the suffering is known to you. A part of you. Kiki's cries would reside in me for years. They still do. This is a part of the hard reality of being a DEA agent. *There are images that cannot be unseen. There are screams that cannot be unheard. And there are things that cannot be undone.* But they are also part of the sacrifice of what it takes to get to the truth. This is something I would have to continuously remind myself during my investigation. As I listened to the tapes over and over and over, trying to pick up something that might have been missed, maybe a fragment of a question or an inference to an event, anything, I also couldn't help but remind myself something else: Something wasn't right.

About all of it.

· · · · ·

Though I wasn't privy to the confidential or sensitive details that previous Leyenda agents had uncovered during their investigations, there was still enough factual and anecdotal information circulating in the agency for me to grasp the generalities of Kiki's murder. The undisputed narrative was that Kiki, while on a routine surveillance flight with a pilot named Alfredo Zavala, had discovered a massive swath of land cultivating thousands of acres of marijuana at a place called Rancho Búfalo in Chihuahua. The ranch was owned by Quintero and Fonseca and was said to represent billions of dollars in revenue for the Guadalajara Cartel. Kiki's discovery of the ranch had led to its raid by the DEA. As a result, members of the Guadalajara Cartel killed him.

While this account could have certainly been true, even before I took over Leyenda I held a number of unstated reservations. There were three primary details of the accepted narrative that seemed uncharacteristic of how the cartel, or even their *pistoleros*, generally operated.

The first detail I found curious was the fact that Kiki was blindfolded. This may seem very minor and perhaps even fundamental to a kidnapping, but having witnessed (and been a part of) dozens of cartel abductions while assigned in Mexico, I had never seen it. Blindfolding an abductee just wasn't a part of the cartel's modus operandi. The drug lords owned Guadalajara. They took who they wanted. They killed who they wanted. And they did so with absolute impunity. Kiki's blindfolding was also curious for another reason. It suggested that the cartel had never intended to kill him. *Why blindfold an abductee if he was to be killed anyway?*

A second and more peculiar facet of the case involved Kiki's interrogation tapes. Their existence had emerged early in the previous investigation courtesy of the CIA who informed the DEA that the Mexican Federal Judicial Police had somehow obtained them. After much political maneuvering and pressure from the U.S. government, the MFJP gave up the tapes to the DEA. But before I had listened to them, I found it strange that they even existed. Again, this was something that wasn't part of what the cartel did or how they operated. There was a specific reason for this: Cartel leaders would be hard-pressed to find a *pistolero* who could have competently manned the recorder. As stunning as this might sound, most *pistoleros* lacked the rudimentary but requisite knowledge to run a tape recorder. Mexico is a third-world country. Guadalajara is the third world of the third world. Most *pistoleros* had very little education, few of whom could even read or write. Given their lack of technical savvy, to run something as simple as a tape recorder would have been akin to calculus for them.

There was something even more concerning about the tapes aside from their mere existence. Of the five tapes that were said to be obtained by the MFJP, only three had been provided to the DEA. And on the three tapes, most was heavily redacted with large portions of the interrogation missing. *What exactly was so important that it had to be erased? And by whom?*

The final aspect of the accepted narrative of Kiki's murder, and the that had probably troubled me the most, involved the discovery of the marijuana fields at Rancho Búfalo and its subsequent raid by the DEA. As massive as this plantation was, it was not nearly the lifeblood of the Guadalajara Cartel that it had been heralded. Illegal marijuana exports to the United States were only around $100 million a year in the mid-1980s. And while Mexico was the leading exporter to the U.S., that total included Colombia, Jamaica, Bolivia and Belize. Compare that to the close to $3 billion the Guadalajara Cartel was netting with their production and distribution of cocaine and heroin. In other words, weed didn't represent that much revenue to the cartel. *It was weed.* This is not to say marijuana wasn't enormously important to them. It was by far their lowest maintenance product. It could be grown pretty much anywhere and needed very little care or cultivation. It was also impervious to inclement weather. *It was weed.* For them it was like "free money," which in turn allowed them to re-invest in their lucrative cocaine and heroin manufacturing. Regardless of the value of the marijuana seized at Rancho Búfalo, to me, it still didn't warrant Kiki's murder. The DEA was constantly involved in massive busts throughout Mexico and South America. Not even a year before the raid at Rancho Búfalo, the DEA seized 13.8 metric tons of Colombian cocaine worth $1.2 billion that was to be distributed by the Guadalajara Cartel. While never pleasing to the drug lords, busts large and small were viewed as nothing more than the cost of doing business. As much as cartel members surely despised the DEA and its agents, there was also an intrinsic understanding that *they were just doing their jobs.*

The most troubling but little known coda to the narrative that Kiki's discovery of the Rancho Búfalo marijuana fields and its subsequent raid were the reason for his murder was an ironic one — *he was not part of either.* Kiki was an incredible agent and a true American hero. But Kiki did not "discover" the fields at Rancho Búfalo with pilot Alfredo Zavala. Kiki and the pilot never actually came near the fields. The pair had discovered another plantation, though not as large, at Zacatecas, Fresnillo. Kiki's discovery of those fields and his methodical investigation which led to its raid is well-documented. The 1,000 hectares of marijuana that made up the Rancho Búfalo fields were never "discovered" by any agent for the simple fact that they were impossible to get to. All roads leading to the plantation were blocked off by the Mexican Judicial Police. Even the sky above the plantation was part of a "no-fly zone." The DEA had only learned of the fields when one of the workers on the plantation, who happened to be a DEA informant, managed to escape and report its existence to the DEA's office in Hermosillo. Rancho Búfalo's bust and seizure was assigned to another agent named Charlie Lugo, who led the raid in November of 1984. *But Kiki was not even there.* This basic fact seemed to be either overlooked by the hierarchy of the agency or completely disregarded.

One final dimension to Kiki's murder that may have only existed as a tertiary footnote to Operation Leyenda, but which would be a bellwether for what I would experience during my investigation, was the U.S. government's stunning, if willful, ignorance about the War on Drugs. They believed unwaveringly that *we were winning it.*

Throughout the greater part of the early 1980s, U.S. officials consistently boasted of their exemplary international cooperation with Mexico in their fight against drug trafficking. They cited bogus statistics. They hailed the success of their aerial crop-eradication program. The White House even claimed that Nancy Reagan's noble-minded but ridiculously unsuccessful "Just Say No" campaign was responsible for a huge decline in demand for narcotics. Toward the end of 1983, after an expensive and exhaustive "study," the House Select Committee on Narcotics Abuse and Control even had the audacity to report, "...*Mexico has been successful in virtually eliminating marijuana production and has substantially reduced opium cultivation.*"

Such bald-faced claims were not merely wrong, they were delusory. Those of us in the DEA and on the front lines of the War on Drugs knew these claims to be a sham, but it took the brazen kidnapping and murder of one of our agents for the American people to realize they may have been duped. Only then did an alternative narrative begin to seep into the public discourse: that the drug war in Mexico was *a nightmare.* Remarkably, even by the time I took over Leyenda in 1989, there still seemed to be a disconnect between those of us in the field of the DEA and officials in Washington.

While the misgivings I held about the accepted narrative of Kiki's murder may not have changed any one of the suspect's likely guilt in the crimes, it did create a fault-line in my own narrative of events — a fault-line I was hoping would be repaired as I continued my investigation.

* * * * *

By the summer of 1989, less than six months after I had taken over Operation Leyenda, the first phase of the investigation was just about complete and it had been nothing short of an absolute success. Through exhaustive research of the previous files coupled with a renewed commitment to bringing those responsible to justice, the investigation had crystallized and we were moving forward on a true bill that would lead to the indictment of 16 of the conspirators involved in Kiki's death. Of the 16, we had already arrested Rubén Zuno Arce. We had even applied enough pressure to the Mexican government to arrest Gallardo. Amazingly, after a four year investigation, Mexican law enforcement discovered that Gallardo was hiding at his home with his family in Guadalajara City.

The next step in the investigation was to have my team begin to build their very strong cases against those guilty of the crimes. While I should have been overjoyed at the progress we were making, I still couldn't help but suspect there might be more to the story of Kiki's murder than was appearing in the surface details. Something I couldn't quite see, but I could feel. *Something dark.* Aside from my original misgivings about the case, I couldn't help but feel that somebody must have provided those responsible with key information on Kiki's schedule and whereabouts prior to his abduction. Another little-known detail that contributed to this feeling was that Kiki was scheduled to be transferred less than two weeks after his abduction. This didn't represent some kind of dramatic irony for me. It suggested that somebody must have known that Kiki's days of working in Guadalajara were coming to an end. *Somebody outed Kiki. Who?*

The first evidence that piqued my interest was the corroborated stories from confidential informants about a peculiar gringo they called "Torre Blanco," the "white tower." The informants said that this Torre Blanco, a tall, light-haired American, was friendly with the drug lords of the Guadalajara Cartel and was often seen at houses belonging to their cartel bosses, including the killing house at 881 Lope de Vega. According to the informants, Torre Blanco was some kind of surveillance and communications expert. They didn't know for sure, but the rumor that had circulated among them was that the gringo's real name was Larry and he was an American who worked for the DFS.

The DFS, or the Dirección Federal de Seguridad, is like our CIA — except that it is exclusively Mexican and male. The mere thought of some white boy from America who was hooked up with them sounded pretty fucking crazy to me. But all the informants' accounts were so consistent I thought they just might be legitimate. So I started working our paid informant network in Mexico, which included DFS agents, seeking out more information about "some gringo named Larry" who worked for the DFS. And sure as shit, I found one. His full name was Lawrence Victor Harrison.

Through my network, I obtained a contact number for Larry Harrison and though I didn't know anything about his involvement in the case, I played it otherwise when I called and left a message for him. I said his name had been implicated in the kidnapping and murder of Kiki Camarena and that I understood he may have some valuable information for which I was willing to pay him a lot of money. I told him I was either going to pay him or bust him. It was his choice, but it was definitely going to be one or the other, so he needed to meet with me.

A few days later, Harrison called me back.

"Agent Berrellez," he said. "This is Larry Harrison. What do you want?"

"Larry," I said. "I told you what I want. I'd like to talk to you."

Harrison didn't even hesitate. "Hector, you have no fucking idea what you are really investigating here. You are in deep and dangerous waters my friend. Good bye."

And he hung up.

• • • • •

My first impression of "Gringo Larry" after that phone call was that he was full of shit. I thought maybe he was just trying to throw me off track. Maybe he was trying to scare me. I didn't know or care. So I called him right back and didn't even let him talk when he picked up.

"Listen, motherfucker. What do you think, *I fell out of a Tule tree?* I know more about this case and who's involved than anybody in the world. And unless you want me to send a few of my contacts to come and grab your ass, you are going to fucking talk to my agents."

After a few minutes of haggling, Gringo Larry agreed to meet with four of my agents at the Lafayette Hotel in Jalisco. I called my agents and informed them. Then, following standard procedure, I notified the DEA office in D.C. that I'd set up a meeting between my agents and a potential confidential informant named Larry Harrison. As Special Agent in Charge of the investigation, I typically did not attend initial interviews. I would leave my agents to vet the potential witnesses. If I felt they could be of value, I would conduct a follow-up interview. In the course of my career investigating cases throughout Mexico, I had set up hundreds of meetings with potential informants and per protocol, I had always notified D.C. Nothing out of the ordinary had ever occurred as a result. Not so with Harrison. Soon after I notified D.C. about the meeting, I received a call from headquarters that a DEA agent named Dale Stinson, who was stationed in Mexico City, was going to fly to Guadalajara to be there at the hotel when my agents met with Harrison. Strange. I never had another agent request to witness one of my interrogations, but my superiors told me this was necessary because Harrison was a U.S. citizen. When the day of the meeting arrived, something else happened that was odd. *Harrison backed out.* Before they were set to meet, Stinson told my agents, "Let me talk to this guy alone first. I have direct orders from DEA country attaché to check this guy out before you interview him."

My agents honored the request and Stinson went into the room to talk with Harrison alone. Five minutes later, when my agents were about to walk in and start their interview, Harrison stepped out.

"I've changed my mind," he said. "I'm not going to cooperate with you and I want nothing to do with you guys." And he left.

What the fuck.

According to my agents, when they asked Stinson what was going on, he told them that he had no idea why Harrison had suddenly changed his mind. After all the bullshit, we got nothing from "Gringo Larry." This only made me more determined to talk to him. So I went after him again. Then something else happened. *Harrison went dark.*

· · · · ·

It's not hard to get lost in Mexico. Long before technology could easily track a person, the country was ideal for disappearance. But if there was one thing I excelled in, it was finding people. During the years I spent in Mexico, I had acquired hundreds of valuable informants from all over the country. I knew the place, people and culture as well as anyone, and finding Larry Harrison would not be my most difficult missing persons. The dude could hide for a while and had he been Mexican, maybe a little longer, but eventually I would find him. And I did. It took me a few weeks to track him down because he had married a local Indian woman and moved into the mountains of the Sierra Madre Occidental. When we finally connected, he sounded almost relieved and agreed to meet with me. But it came with caveats. He would only meet on American soil. And it would have to be in secret. He said, "Hector, I don't want anybody there to know who I am and don't tell anybody that I'm coming. And you need to get me into the country secretly or you will put both our lives at risk. *Do you fucking understand?*"

I gave him my word that I would abide by those terms.

I then called an agent in Sonora and arranged for one of our jets to secretly fly Harrison from the Hermosillo Airport to Los

Angeles under protection from the DEA. As soon as Harrison heard about this, he called me.

"Are you out of your fucking mind, Berrellez? I'm not flying out of Hermosillo. It's too public. Find an airstrip outside the city."

I said, "Sure, no problem," thinking this guy better be worth it, because he was sure becoming a pain in my ass. I redirected the pilots to a small dirt airstrip outside Imuris, Sonora.

The thing about small airstrips is they're really not suitable for jets. They're built for small cargo planes, those flying tin cans used by small-time smugglers. When my agent went out there to wait with Harrison for his ride, they watched in horror as the jet overshot the small patch of dirt and crashed right in front of them.

This was a big problem. Harrison was now freaking out. Meanwhile, I had to call the head of the DEA in Mexico, Country Attaché Ralph Saucedo, to tell him we needed agents to guard the scene and figure out how to clear the wreckage because the plane was totaled. Ralph was mad as hell. Remember, he had no idea I had been doing any of this. I had been operating on my own. On top of cleaning up that mess, I had to figure out a way to get Harrison into the U.S. I was going to try to arrange for another flight somewhere in Sonora, but that would have been a logistical nightmare on such short notice. Plus, it would mean too many calls and I was still trying to keep the operation under wraps. So I said, fuck it. We'll just drive Gringo Larry to the U.S. I arranged to put him and the pilots in a car and ordered them driven to the U.S. port of entry in Nogales, Arizona. I remained emphatic to my agents — under no circumstances is Harrison to be identified.

When their car arrived at the point of entry a few hours later, my agent showed the customs supervisor his DEA badge and said,

"We cannot identify this man. He's an anonymous witness in a major DEA investigation."

The customs supervisor said, "I don't care who you are or who he is, I'm not letting an unidentified individual into the U.S. from Mexico."

My agent called me up. At this point, it had already been a hell of a long day. He put me on the phone with the customs supervisor who was acting like a grade A hard ass. I identified myself as the leader of a special DEA task force and told him that I really needed him to allow this individual into the U.S. anonymously as it was critical to the investigation of a major crime.

"You identify him for us, and we'll let him in," the customs guy said.

"I can't do that."

"Okay, then he's not coming in.".

Motherfucker.

"We'll see about that," I replied.

And I called Jack Lawn.

"Mr. Lawn, I'm having a problem. I have a major witness, a U.S. citizen, with a lot of explosive information about the Camarena case. I personally guaranteed him that I would not identify him to any U.S. government authorities and I need to keep that promise. But U.S. Customs at the Nogales port of entry won't let him in without knowing his identity."

Jack Lawn called the Director of Customs and Immigration, who in turn called the supervisor at Nogales and said, "Let him in." I'm not a guy that likes pulling rank, but I would have loved to see that smug customs supervisor's face as my agents breezed past him with my undocumented witness.

By this point, Harrison was about to shit his pants. He was already freaked out over the plane crash and he sure as hell didn't want to spend another seven hours on the road driving from Nogales to Los Angeles. He wanted to stay right there in Arizona. So I had to send another DEA plane to pick him up. Harrison got on the plane for the short flight but when it landed in L.A., the plane blew a tire and skidded like mad all over the runway. When Harrison got off the plane, my task force agents were there to meet him and he was fuming.

"What kind of bullshit operation do you motherfuckers run?" he said. "First I'm driving from Guadalajara to Hermosillo. Then I'm almost run over by a fucking plane that crashes in on top of us. Then I'm driving all the way to Nogales where I'm nearly arrested by U.S. customs. Then the second plane crash lands. What the fuck?"

I was actually preparing to meet with him that evening but when my agents called to tell me what kind of mood he was in, I changed my mind.

"Get him a good steak and take him to a nice hotel and watch him," I said, feeling sorry for him. "We'll do the interview tomorrow."

They took him to a nice steakhouse then put him up in the Embassy Suites off the I-10 Freeway. Poor bastard.

The next morning I went to the hotel with one of my agents, Wayne Schmidt, to interview Harrison. Finally, I thought, we're going to get this guy to talk. By then, I'd been on CNN and network news talking about the Camarena case, so when I started to introduce myself, he said, "I know who you are. Everybody in Mexico knows who you are."

"Okay, here's the deal," I said. "I know that you spent time at the house in Guadalajara where Kiki Camarena was tortured and murdered. I have witnesses who say you were with those drug traffickers on many occasions. What I don't know is why?"

Harrison looked at me like I had spoken Mandarin. "You don't know anything, do you, Hector? You're just runnin' around, waving your dick like a big shot, buying this informant and that informant when all you gotta do is follow the money."

"What the hell are you talking about?"

"I'm talking about Camarena," he said. "You still don't know why he was even picked up or who sold him out."

This was a half-truth. I thought I knew why, or least I knew the accepted narrative, the narrative believed by the cartel. The fields at Rancho Búfalo. "I know why, Larry. But you are right, I don't know who sold him out. Why don't you tell me?"

Through all my conversations with Larry Harrison, until I had met him in person, I always felt that he treated me with a degree of arrogance. He was alternatively rude, dismissive, entitled. But having asked him that question, for the first time, I saw him look me over with another emotion. Sympathy. He held that look for a while as he thought to himself, even repeating the question as if stunned by the very ignorance of it.

"You wanna know who sold Kiki Camarena out, Hector?"

I did. But never in my wildest imagination was I prepared for his answer.

"*We did.*"

I looked at him, incredulous. "Who's we?"

"The U.S. government that you and I work for."

I sat stunned for a long moment, just staring at him. His initial expression of sympathy quickly gave way to contempt.

"Duh..." he said, as if speaking to an imbecile. "Hector, I work for the CIA. How stupid are you?"

That question echoed inside of my head. *How stupid was I? What had I not seen? What did I not understand? What was the bigger picture?*

As I tried to make sense of this, Harrison got angry. "First you contact me and ask me to cooperate with you on the Camarena murder. The next thing I know, I'm talking with another CIA agent at the meeting you set up who orders me not to cooperate with you and threatens to report me."

He was talking about DEA agent Dale Stinson, who had been sent to the Lafayette Hotel to sit in on the original meeting.

"What?! Stinson is in the CIA?"

"Of course he is, you dumb ass. The CIA has dozens of agents in Mexico. They work in every agency."

I was speechless. Harrison slowed it down for me. "Look," he said. "The CIA runs the DFS. How else do you think I could have gotten a job there? And do you think for one fucking second the DFS is going to kidnap a U.S. federal agent without the CIA knowing about it first?"

He was right. But I still couldn't believe it.

"You're telling me that our government, the U.S. government, was involved in Kiki's abduction and murder?" I asked again.

"That's exactly what I'm telling you. I know all about Kiki Camarena. I know why they picked him up. I know why they killed him. I know everything about it and how deep it goes."

I took a deep breath. My mind shouldn't have had any trouble processing what Harrison was telling me. I was, at the end of the day, a cop. An investigator. I was trained to look at all cases from every angle until each of the pieces came into place. And I knew the narrative that Kiki had been killed because of his discovery of Rancho Búfalo was faulty. But there was another part of me that had a very difficult time reconciling what I was hearing. *My spirit.*

Throughout my professional life I had firmly believed that despite its many flaws, our country was unimpeachable. We were righteous and we were always on the right side of justice. I believed in the American ideal. It was something firmly imprinted into my Spanish, Mexican and Catholic DNA. If there was one article of faith at the very core of my belief system, it was that America was good.

I was about to go down a road where I would find out that was no longer true.

Chapter 18

Sigue el dinero
Follow the Money

Harrison's claims hit me like a sucker punch, but I still remained quite incredulous. *I could not believe him.* Per protocol, we wrote up our report and submitted it, but I also called D.C. and let them know that I had found a potential witness who was either going to blow Operation Leyenda out of the water — or was out of his fucking mind. I wasn't sure which one. They weren't sure either but they suggested I fly Harrison to D.C. and they would have him "boxed," which was a colloquial we used for polygraphing witnesses. I tried to place him aside, wait for the results of his test and get back to the rest of the case that was moving forward. But I couldn't completely let go of him. As skeptical as I was about his story, there was one particular thing he said that really resonated with me. That was, *"Follow the money."* I didn't know what money he was talking about. *Did the Guadalajara Cartel pay to have Kiki kidnapped? Was Kiki given money by the cartel? Did Kiki find any money?*

At that point in the investigation, despite Harrison's outrageous claims, all evidence still pointed to the fact that the leaders of the Guadalajara Cartel had acted on their own. There was not a shred of proof that had suggested otherwise. As far as Kiki being given money was concerned, I had considered this. It was not out of the realm of comprehension that he could have been on the cartel's payroll. Every agent in the field is vulnerable to temptation and, unfortunately, some have fallen prey to those temptations. However, I would have bet my life that Kiki wasn't one of them. The DEA is a brotherhood.

Most field agents either know each other or *know of* each other. While I didn't know Kiki well, I made my career reading and understanding people. This was more often than not a "gut feeling." It came from years of experience in the field and studying human behavior and psychology. There was also a spiritual aspect involved. Based on all of these, I knew that *Kiki was good.* But as I thought about this, I also remembered a particular sequence in the interrogation tapes when an infuriated Quintero asked Kiki about "his money."

"*What about the money you stole!?*" Quintero yelled.

Kiki's answer in between beatings was, "I don't know anything about any money."

Interestingly, this was one of the many sequences on the tapes that was redacted immediately following an exchange.

Was this the money Harrison was talking about? And where was it given? I didn't know. *Was there money that Kiki had found?* I knew that answer. There was. A lot of it. That I knew to be true. Maybe that was the money Harrison was talking about. *Maybe that was the money I was supposed to follow.*

It certainly would have made sense. For the drug lords of the Guadalajara Cartel, as with all drug lords, there is a big difference between losing product and losing money. Drug lords expect to lose product. They see lost product as a cost of doing business. But when you fuck with a drug lord's money? That is another thing entirely. Fresh from what I believed to be somewhat of an epiphany in my investigation, I received a phone call from the administrator's office in Washington. Jack Lawn wanted to meet with me. *Privately.*

Chapter 19

Secuestrar
To Kidnap

To be personally requested by the administrator of the DEA for an appointment — clandestinely — was anything but DEA protocol. I thought it may have been to brief him on my new findings in Kiki's case, but I quickly learned it was for something else. Without wasting any time, Lawn began the meeting with a question.

"Hector, could you kidnap a Mexican national from his own country?"

Hmm. Of course I could. It was Mexico. Anything was possible. So I said to him, "Mr. Lawn, you give me enough money, I can kidnap the president of Mexico."

He smiled at me. "Good. Because I want you to kidnap Dr. Machaín for his role in Kiki's murder."

Machaín had been the doctor who injected lidocaine into Kiki's heart to keep him alive during his interrogation. I sat there for a moment, incredulous. The idea of abducting a foreign national wasn't unheard of. It was called "extraterritorial rendition" and officially/unofficially gave the green light to U.S. federal law enforcement to arrest foreign nationals suspected of terrorism. But Dr. Machaín was no ordinary Mexican national. He was one of the key professionals in the Guadalajara Cartel. In reality, kidnapping him would be a hell of a lot more difficult than kidnapping the president of Mexico — and probably more expensive. I also wasn't clear if Dr. Machaín fit the legal definition of a foreign terrorist. Kidnapping him could make me a criminal, so I expressed my concerns on both fronts. Lawn assured me that we were on solid legal ground.

"I want that man, Hector, for what he did to Kiki. " Lawn studied me and leaned in. *"Can you do this, Hector?"*

Again, there was no question as to *if I could do it.* The question he was really asking was, *would I do it?* And my answer to both of these would be the same.

Fuck yes.

* * * * *

It wasn't the first time I had been asked to kidnap a Mexican national. During my time as Resident Agent in Charge in Mazatlán, I received a similar request to "displace" another high-level associate of the Guadalajara Cartel. The request had come from Pete Gruden, who was with the Office of Professional Responsibility (OPR), and it came under the most emphatic order of non-disclosure.

I gave him my word that I would keep the operation dark. I reached out to a *comandante* I knew and trusted and told him the plan. Given the level of the target's profile within the cartel, the *comandante* was reluctant. I promised him he would be paid and that all he had to do was deliver us the target. The DEA would take care of the rest. We agreed to work together, put together a plan and in less than 24 hours it was done. The *comandante* confirmed it with a phone call.

"I have your package."

"Fantastic," I said. "Let me arrange the transfer."

I thought that was it. But that transfer would never take place. Not even an hour upon hearing from the *comandante* I received another phone call, this one from Ed Heath, the DEA's country attaché.

"Hector," he said. "Were you planning on kidnapping someone?"

"Who wants to know?"

"Pilliod wants to know about it for one."

He was referring to U.S. Ambassador to Mexico Charles Pilliod. How he found out about it was anyone's guess.

"Look, Hector," he said. "Whatever you have planned, abort it."

"I can't do that, Ed. It's already done."

"Well, then undo it!" he snapped before hanging up.

I called Pete Gruden at OPR. "Pete. We have a problem with that package you asked for."

"What's the problem?"

"I just got off the phone with Ed Heath. Pilliod found out about it. He wants me to abort."

"Goddammit," he said, trying to think what our options were.

"Pete. I can't abort. We already have the package."

"What?! How did you get him so fast?"

"I don't fuck around, Ed."

"Apparently not. I guess you have to set him free."

I sighed. This was an impossibility. "Ed, you know I can't do that. If he's set free, the *comandante* I hired and all his men are dead."

"Hector, if Pilliod knows about it and wants the plug pulled, that's where it ends. I'm sorry."

Fuck.

I called the *comandante* back and set a time and place to meet with him as soon as possible. He was more than accommodating because he thought he was going to get paid. But when I showed up at our arranged place of meeting holding nothing but a bottle of top-shelf tequila, he knew something was up. I got right to the point.

"I'm sorry, *comandante*, but there has been a change in plans."

"What kind of change?"

"You need to let the package go."

The *comandante's* face went blank. "Are you out of your fucking mind, Berrellez? I can't do that."

I shrugged helplessly. He was 100% correct. There was no way he could simply let "the package" go free. He, as well as his men and many of their family members, would be killed instantly.

"I'm sorry," I said. And I meant it.

The *comandante* looked at me with disdain.

"Americans. You do whatever you want with your stupid War on Drugs and don't give a damn about us." He got up and walked away. I didn't blame him.

The target was not "set free." He disappeared like so many of the other targets in our "stupid War on Drugs."

The whole episode always left a bad taste in my mouth about "black ops." Not only did that operation cost me a lot of hard-earned cachet with the Mexican *comandante*, as well as those he employed, the situation had also cost someone their life. Yes, I know the target had been a drug trafficker and a very bad person, but he was still a citizen and entitled to his due process. In the DEA, we were taught to investigate and prosecute. We did not act as judge and jury. We did not adjudicate. And we definitely didn't exterminate.

• • • • •

By the time my flight from D.C. landed back at LAX, the true gravity of Administrator Jack Lawn's request finally hit me. My immediate reaction to any challenge, risk or threat had always been constant: all in. I got right to work putting together the nucleus of the plan to "displace" Dr. Machaín. No matter where a DEA agent is stationed in Mexico, the local cops are the key to a successful mission. They help with logistics. They give you access to the target. And they provide cover and muscle. They're not just the cornerstone of the operation, they're its lifeblood. So I started with the police officials who I knew could be bought.

First to mind was Ignacio Barragán Maldonado. Ignacio was one of my best contacts in all of Mexico. As a former high-ranking Federal Judicial Police *comandante* and a relative of former Mexico Secretary of Defense Marcelino Garcia Barragán, he was the perfect combination of corruption, connection and greed. Together, he and I gathered a crack squad of police and military officers. Considering this was Mexico, you always need a little more in case things go sideways. Because in Mexico, they always go sideways. So we hired a ragtag group of local mercenaries and common Guadalajara criminals who we called "the Wild Geese," named after the old

Richard Burton, Roger Moore movie. Between all of us, we probably could have pulled off a coup of the Mexican government.

On April 3, 1990, we used two attractive young women to entice Dr. Machaín to his medical clinic. Once he was inside, we had the Wild Geese rush in and take the doctor captive. With Ignacio's police and other paid military paving the way, Dr. Machaín was extracted from the clinic without incident. He was thrown into a waiting car, transported to Leon, Guanajuato, put on a Turbo Aero Commander plane and flown directly to El Paso, Texas where I placed him under federal arrest. Two weeks later, Dr. Machaín appeared before a U.S. magistrate in Los Angeles. A grand jury was convened and indicted him for complicity in the abduction, torture and murder of Kiki Camarena.

Boom.

It had been done. I was euphoric. We bagged one of the major players in the Camarena murder investigation, and I was now convinced that we had moved the case forward with such a major victory that the other co-conspirators' days were numbered. My euphoric feelings didn't last long. Shortly after the kidnapping, a contact in D.C. called me. The results of "Gringo Larry" Harrison's polygraph had come in. He passed.

Larry Harrison was telling the truth.

Chapter 20

Veintitrés
Twenty-three

The thought of my own government's involvement in Kiki's death was something I still couldn't comprehend. In my head, I was at a stage of absolute denial. And despite the trickle of evidence I had begun to uncover that challenged the accepted narrative of events, Kiki's lack of participation in the Rancho Búfalo raid, the dubious interrogation tapes and Quintero's rage regarding stolen money, *I still did not want to believe Larry Harrison.* I wanted the case to be clean and clear. The previous investigative teams had given me plenty of forensic evidence that provided me with a whole lot of facts. But *I still didn't know the truth.* I would never really know what happened to Kiki at Lope de Vega until I talked to someone *who was actually there.* I needed someone who was *in that room with Kiki.* I needed someone who *heard it all. Saw it all.* I needed to find an eyewitness.

I was not Leyenda's first agent to aggressively pursue eyewitnesses. It had been attempted by the previous investigative teams. But as I would quickly discover, if providing material witnesses in Mexico was dangerous, working as a criminal informant on Operation Leyenda was nothing shy of a death sentence. When I tried to reestablish a dialogue with some of my previous informants about the case, I was met with a wall of silence. Most would no longer return my calls. I discovered why after I managed to track down one of my more loyal informants, and was relieved to find out he was willing to meet and tell me what he knew. But the meeting never took place. Shortly after I had arranged for the informant's travel to Los Angeles, he went missing. Sometime later, I received a phone call from an intermediary who told me the informant had been found with his little boy. Both had been brutally tortured and murdered. The little boy's testicles had been burned off with a blow-torch.

It was only fate that could have steered me toward my first key witness. Of all people in my past it would involve, it was my best friend and college bandmate, Arturo Meyer, who would be the thread that brought us together. Over the holidays late in 1989, I had been invited to a wedding back in South Tucson for an old friend of my family's. Weddings are a big deal to my family and Mexican culture and I always looked forward to them as a "reunion" with all the people I had grown up with. One of the guests at this wedding was a man named Antonio Gárate Bustamante. He looked awfully familiar to me. Thing is, I noticed he too was staring me down. When I went to say hello to Mrs. Meyer, I asked her, *who is this guy?*

"You two should know each other," she said.

"And why is that?"

"Because he used to be a *comandante* for the Jalisco State Police."

"And why is he at your table?"

"Because he's Arturo's uncle."

It was true. Antonio Bustamante was not only Art's uncle, as former *comandante* for the Jalisco police he had also been one of the most well-informed men in all of Guadalajara with deep connections within the cartel. In fact, Ernesto Fonseca Carrillo was the *padrino de bodas*, or best man, at his wedding. Bustamante had been flipped by the DEA before I began my assignment in Mazatlán and was working as an informant in Phoenix.

The *comandante* and I buckled up to the bar, ordered more than a few shots of tequila, swapped stories and got along famously. Bustamante knew everyone I needed to know. After a few more shots of tequila we became fast friends. After a few more, I asked him to come to Los Angeles to work with me on Leyenda. He accepted. Had we had more shots, I might have invited him to move in with me, my wife and kids.

Antonio Bustamante proved to be a real ace in the hole for the investigation. Though he didn't know of anyone who was directly involved in Kiki's murder, he did know someone *who might be:* a young man whose family owned a string of brothels in Guadalajara and supplied the prostitutes for parties thrown by the cartel's drug lords. The young man's name was Rafa. Bustamante introduced me to Rafa and the young man agreed to work with me.

Over the course of my career as a DEA agent, I have squeezed, cajoled, convinced and even paid hundreds if not a thousand men or women to offer up their services as informant or witness against those I was trying to apprehend. It didn't take a lot of savvy when I worked on the U.S. side of the border. Most of the time, the criminal informant was left with no choice.

Given the option of a reduced sentence or no sentence at all in exchange for some testimony, any criminal will choose the latter.

Surprisingly, many other CIs actually *volunteer their services.* Sometimes it's to eliminate a rival. Other times it's for revenge. There are even times, though rare, when a criminal has a moment of clarity and feels the moral compunction to "do the right thing." None of these reasons or scenarios are ever in play in Mexico. Mexicans are both fiercely tribal and loyal. It is not part of the Mexican DNA to betray one of their own. There is the omnipresent, unseeable dark cloud of *fear* that permeates every aspect of life in Mexico. In urban areas across the U.S., "snitches get stitches" is a popular street idiom. In Mexico, snitches are not so lucky. In Mexico, snitches get caskets — if they're found at all. In Mexico, giving material witness against members of a cartel puts one's own life at risk, but many times it also puts the lives of one's family and friends at risk.

I went to great lengths to protect all of my criminal informants. Unfortunately, the reach and power we stood against was often greater than the security I could provide. I remember having such a conversation with Rafa while he was under the DEA's protective services up near Big Bear in Southern California. He had been housed there for a while before he decided to work with me on the investigation. Given the gravity of the case, we spent a considerable amount of time together and developed a personal relationship. I came to know him quite well and discovered he was an incredibly good-hearted person whose only crime was being born in Guadalajara. Though he was surrounded by violence for much of his 20+ years of life, he detested it and never even owned a gun. The kid did not drink, smoke or even swear. We became great friends and I even used to bring my son to see him as well. The two were like little kids. They would play video games, order pizza and laugh with each other. After a few months of this, the pangs of missing his family and his home began to overwhelm him. He wanted to leave. Rafa had done more for me and Operation Leyenda than I could have ever hoped for. But I wanted him to stay. I told him it was too dangerous and that if he went home, he would be killed. Rafa knew this. But he chose to go home anyway.

"I have to see my family," he said.

I don't know if Rafa ever did. After he left our protection and went back to Mexico, Rafa was never seen or heard from again.

• • • • •

I do not take the gift of life lightly. While I am haunted by all the life lost as a result of my actions, it may be the loss of the informants I recruited and used throughout my career who haunt me the most. At the same time I am equally as grateful to them. None of my criminal informants died in vain. Because of them, innumerable cases were moved forward and a countless number of bad people were put in prison. All of the most critical knowledge I gained about Kiki's murder was gained from Rafa. He would be the 23rd informant who was killed for working with me.

PART FOUR

DEATH

This is the way the world ends, not with a bang, but a whimper.

–T.S. Eliot, "The Hollow Men"

Chapter 21

Arbusto ardiente
Burning Bush

Author's Note: There are certain elements of the abduction, torture and murder of Kiki Camarena that cannot be disclosed at this time. The DEA's investigation is still ongoing and case agents are still interviewing and pursuing new witnesses to glean new information. While much of what will be revealed in the following chapters may be new, the majority of my revelations have been documented through a variety of sources.

· · · · ·

It was with Rafa's help that I zeroed in on prospective eyewitnesses, including a man named Jorge Godoy. Though Godoy was born in Guadalajara, through my research I discovered he was actually raised in America and had attended high school in Los Angeles. Godoy had wanted to be a soldier in the U.S. Army, but he was rejected because he didn't have immigration papers and was sent back to Guadalajara. There, a friend who worked in the state attorney's office helped him get a job with the Jalisco State Police. What Godoy didn't realize was that working for the state police in Guadalajara meant you were really working for the Guadalajara

Cartel. On the first day of his job, Godoy's *comandante* took him to a club where he introduced him to the heads of the cartel, Quintero and Fonseca.

"These guys are your new bosses," the *comandante* told Godoy.

Fonseca quickly took to Godoy, who was big, charismatic and had been raised in the states. *"Estás conmigo, yanquee,"* he said, which means, *you're with me, Yankee*. And that was it. Two days later, Godoy moved into Fonseca's mansion and began full-time duty as his bodyguard — 24 hours a day, 7 days a week, 365 days a year.

There was no doubt in my mind that Godoy would have been privy to everything the cartel was involved in. Having learned of him, my instincts told me he could be flipped. Something told me, *he was good.* Through Bustamante's network, I arranged to have Godoy sent to Los Angeles on a bogus assignment where I would meet with him.

I picked Godoy up at the San Isidro port of entry, introduced myself and drove him north from San Diego to a safe house in Big Bear. As soon as were out of the city and into the mountainous country, Godoy began quivering with fear. He assumed I was taking him somewhere to be executed. In the world he came from, that is what happened to so many people he knew who were on the payroll of drug lords. He was so fearful I thought he might jump out of our moving car, so I pulled over. Godoy was sweating profusely.

"Jorge," I said. "Do you know why I asked to see you?"

Godoy shook his head.

"I want you to work with me. I want you to help me bring justice to those who were involved in killing Kiki Camarena."

Godoy thought about it. "How can I trust you?"

I studied him a moment, looked into his eyes and noticed he was clutching a rosary.

"Do you believe in God, Jorge?" I asked him.

"I do."

"I also believe in God. I am a very religious person, and I swear to God, if you help me I will pay you. I will make sure you and your family are safe. And you will not be arrested."

Godoy met my stare. I didn't need to wait for his answer. I knew it already. *He was in.*

"Now, how much do you know about Kiki Camarena's kidnapping and murder?" I asked.

Godoy hesitated a long moment. Finally, he answered. "*Sé todo lo, comandante,*" he said.

I know everything.

• • • • •

Jorge Godoy knew *almost everything.* As Fonseca's primary bodyguard, he had been at the drug lord's side for every pre-abduction meeting and was privy to the most intimate details of the cartel's plans. What made Godoy an even more valuable witness was that not only did he see almost everything, he also *heard almost everything.* He was fluent in both Spanish *and English.* Most of the key players at the highest levels of drug trafficking often spoke English when discussing business. They did this for the precise reason of keeping their affairs secret in front of those who worked for them, most of whom were poor and uneducated. As I would discover, Godoy's bilingualism allowed him a unique understanding of the event.

According to him, serious talk of Kiki's abduction had begun in the fall of 1984, almost four months before the event took place. He told me the first meeting happened at Las Americas hotel in Guadalajara. In attendance was Manuel Bartlett Diáz, the Secretary of Government, the second most powerful political office in Mexico, which oversees many federal security agencies including the DFS. Bartlett was in charge of DFS activities all over Mexico. Also in attendance was Mexico's Secretary of Defense, General Arévalo Gardoqui, and the head of Interpol in Mexico, Miguel Aldana Ibarra. The governor of Jalisco was also there, along with the local commanders of the state and federal police, plus military officers and the following drug traffickers: Gallardo, Quintero, Cochi Loco, Zuno and Fonseca. Dozens of bodyguards were present, including Godoy, who guarded the door to the suite where the meeting took place and, incidentally, also went into the room multiple times to resupply the men inside with cocaine, drinks and snacks.

Godoy overheard the Secretary of Defense, Arévalo Gardoqui, tell the others that the DEA was applying heavy pressure on the Mexican military to destroy marijuana fields. Bartlett at the time was the ruling Institutional Revolutionary Party (PRI) favorite to become the next president of Mexico. Godoy overheard Bartlett say he was concerned about the DFS credentials and protection he had provided to the drug lords in the room because it could give his political rivals ammunition to use against him if the DEA continued making a big deal about drug traffickers being protected by the Mexican government. The meeting ended with the men agreeing that this "out of control" DEA agent, meaning Kiki Camarena, needed to either be bribed or killed.

The second meeting took place in late November 1984. Godoy remembered that Quintero was in a rage, yelling at the governor of Jalisco that the DEA agent who was taking their money and raiding marijuana plantations needed to be identified and "taken care of" immediately. Godoy recalled that Fonseca had tried to calm the situation down by presenting the governor of Jalisco with a gold-plated AK-47, as both a gift and a bribe.

Not long after that, in December 1984, Godoy recalled being on a security patrol around the perimeter of one of Fonseca's houses when he noticed a white man, clearly an American, installing some kind of device on the telephone pole behind the house. He ran to tell Fonseca, but the drug lord said, "Don't worry, that American is working for us." Larry Harrison sprang to my mind — and it was confirmed when Godoy told me that he and many of the cartel's bodyguards would come to call him "Gringo Larry." But Godoy also mentioned that there had been another white American man who he had seen with Fonseca on occasion. Godoy didn't know who he was and assumed him to be another associate of the cartel bosses. Godoy had reported seeing the white American receive money on at least one occasion. While this certainly gave me pause, I had nowhere to go with it since it could not be corroborated. I also had no idea who it could have been. I even reached out to a few of my other sources to see if anyone else had seen an additional white American orbiting around the cartel's circles, but I heard nothing and Godoy's story died on the vine for the time being.

Another strange aspect of Godoy's story arose when he mentioned that a Cuban man had begun to appear around the ranch, introduced to him as "Max Gomez." At the last pre-abduction meeting, Godoy heard Fonseca tell Bartlett and the Cuban, "We are doing what we said we would do. Now we are waiting for you to do what you said you would do." Then Fonseca told Godoy to help Bartlett and the Cuban carry a stack of cardboard boxes full of cash out to waiting vehicles. The boxes contained about $400 million in cash — more than two tons. Godoy overheard conversations between Fonseca and the Cuban about the money going to support the Nicaraguan Contras, though he didn't know anything about that. But he did hear the men say these "Contras" were being trained at a secret base that Quintero owned in the Mexican state of Veracruz.

I did some digging to see where Kiki might have fit into all of this.

• • • • •

According to the records of Kiki's investigations, he had learned about several huge marijuana plantations that Quintero owned in the north central Mexican state of Zacatecas. Quintero had paid a *comandante* in the Mexican military 50 million pesos to buy the ranches and to place the plantations under military protection. On May 11, 1984, about ten months before he was killed, Kiki learned that Quintero had arrived in Fresnillo, Zacatecas in a convoy of nine vans and fifteen Mercury Grand Marquis luxury sedans. He was traveling with 60 agents from the DFS, the Mexican federal police agency that was trained by the CIA and worked closely with them on covert operations in Mexico.

That same month, Kiki and a Mexican pilot, Alfredo Zavala Avelar, searched for the drug cartel plantations from the air and pinned down their exact locations. At Kiki's insistence, the DEA began pressuring the Mexican state and federal government to take action. Finally, the Mexican authorities raided the plantations. They seized 20 tons of marijuana and enough seed to plant 6,500 acres. They also made 177 arrests, but all the guys they busted were field hands and low-level armed guards. The Mexican police had tipped off Quintero. As mentioned previously, Kiki had been incorrectly attributed to the subsequent discovery of the marijuana fields at Rancho Búfalo. I thought that perhaps the cartel had just conflated the two busts because there was no mention of the Zacatecas raid in any of the interrogation tapes. Then I discovered something interesting.

Before the raid at Rancho Búfalo, Kiki had changed tactics. Instead of going after the product, he went after the money, utilizing what the DEA called "Operation Padrino," which gave the agency the ability to freeze millions and millions of dollars in secret drug-fueled bank accounts throughout the U.S. and Europe. Kiki had stumbled onto some accounts that had been connected to the Veracruz ranch belonging to Quintero. If that were true, he would have been seizing money that was training the Contras in their illegal war. It was at that moment I believed *this* had been the money that Larry Harrison wanted me to "follow".

I had mined Jorge Godoy for every piece of information I could use to put this puzzle in place, but there was one thing that limited the scope of his knowledge. Though he had heard everything leading up to the fateful event, he had not been part of Kiki's abduction, torture and murder. When the date of the kidnapping arrived, Godoy wanted no part of it and did not show up for work that day, citing an "illness." He was invaluable, but I would never have full knowledge of what happened until I found another witness — someone who was actually *in the room when Kiki was tortured and interrogated.* No one at the DEA had yet to produce an actual eyewitness. A man named Ramon Lira would be the first.

Lira had grown up wanting to be a priest. However, he would end up marrying his childhood sweetheart and following in his brother's footsteps, which led to him working as a police officer in Jalisco. Like Godoy, while working as a policeman, he had been chosen to be a bodyguard for Fonseca in 1983. At first, the job was nothing more than moonlighting and Lira, like most family men in Mexico, could use the extra money. But his part-time job for Fonseca eventually became both a full-time job and all-consuming. It also got to the point where he worked solely for Fonseca and rarely checked in with his police department.

In the months leading to Kiki's kidnapping, Lira had also been present at the pre-abduction meetings. Like Godoy, he too had reported seeing a white American who had been with Fonseca. When Lira inquired about the man, Fonseca told him he was a "friend from the DEA." In Mexico, it is not earth-shattering to those who work with cartels to come across crooked or dirty policemen. The general perception among most cartel *pistoleros* is that all lawmen on both sides of the border are crooked. In other words, when Lira heard this, he didn't think twice about it. This was a fact of life in Guadalajara. Substantiating his belief, he recalled an occasion in late 1984 when Fonseca ordered him to go to the trunk of a Grand Marquis and get a half million dollars for the white American "friend" from the DEA.

Okay. Now I had another piece of information. And I had corroboration of a white American — who I was told was a friend of the cartel from the DEA.

What.

The.

Fuck.

This was a potential game-changer. With an accusation so explosive, I couldn't really believe it. If it were true, it would have literally destroyed the DEA. *He had to be mistaken.* But both of my witnesses — and a third, another cartel bodyguard named Rene Lopez — stood by their claims and all told me independently: *There was a white American associated with the DEA who was a friend of the cartel who received money.* Was this who outed Kiki?

I could not write up a DEA-6 for this. I had to be careful. Even a whiff of it would bring down a shit-storm from OPR and potentially interfere with my investigation. So instead, I made a note of this in personal memorandum, forms that the DEA used at times because they are internal and not subject to subpoena. I also began to think long and hard about who exactly could have been this "friend from the DEA." In what was a very odd twist in a case that would continue to have them in spades, I discovered that there was a DEA agent in Guadalajara who had come to the defense of one of the cartel's conspirators in the crimes against Kiki, the conspirator who also happened to be my first arrest while heading Leyenda: Rubén Zuno Arce. In the report, the agent stunningly declared that he knew of no evidence that Zuno was part of a cartel, and that he was a man of integrity. I nearly fell out of my chair when I read it. The following is the DEA-6 written up by the investigating agent:

```
U.S. Department of Justice
Drug Enforcement Administration

                    REPORT OF INVESTIGATION
1. PROGRAM CODE        2. CROSS   RELATED FILES   3. FILE NO.              4. G-DEP IDENTIFIER
                          FILE                    PRTB-85-0032             PE4-CI
5. BY                                             6. FILE TITLE
   Los Angeles, CA                                OPERATION LEYENDA

7. [ ]Closed [ ]Requested Action Completed        8. DATE PREPARED
   [ ]Action Requested By:                        June 4, 1991
9. OTHER OFFICERS:

10. REPORT RE: Bail Hearing for Ruben ZUNO-Arce, 5/31/91

DETAILS:

1. On May 31, 1991, U.S. District Court Judge Edward Rafeedy held a bail hearing for
defendant Ruben ZUNO-Arce pending a retrial in case CR-87-422(F)ER.

2. Judge Rafeedie ordered detention for ZUNO-Arce and the following points were covered by
the court, defense attorney Edward Medvene and AUSA John Carlton.

DEFENSE ARGUMENT FOR BAIL

a) Since the previous bail hearings there have been major changes in the circumstances
   of Mr. ZUNO to warrant bail. This is noticed by both (PSA) pretrial services and the
   court. Additionally the prosecution has failed to present the court with any
   credible evidence to continue to detain ZUNO, there had been no clear and convincing
   evidence presented as required by statute.

b) In addition, ███████████████████████████████████, both of who worked on the
   investigation of his kidnapping have filed declarations saying they know of no
   evidence that ZUNO was part of a cartel or involved in anyway with the kidnapping.

c) Mr. ZUNO is a man of integrity and truthfulness and close family ties.

d) Mr. ZUNO has always come back, always returned for all hearings. Mr. ZUNO is a man
   of his word. All factors concerning the statute point to bail for the defendant.

e) The book mentioned by the prosecutor "Los Caciques" defaming Mr. ZUNO is not
   competent it was written by a political enemy of his.
```

While it was certainly true agents often align themselves with criminals and even protect criminal informants, under no circumstances would an agent — or any lawman for that matter —

testify on behalf of a drug trafficker who was alleged to be a co-conspirator of a federal agent. At the very minimum, this should have been immediate cause for an OPR investigation. As I considered this shocking betrayal, I became convinced that *this had to be the "DEA agent" my witnesses had mentioned.*

I went through the entire case and its files, writing out fastidious memos, but before I turned them in, I focused my attention on the mysterious Cuban known as "Max Gomez." I was hoping he could provide the link between the CIA and the DEA. The only way I could do that was if I found out what exactly happened to Kiki at Lope de Vega. Ramon Lira was there the day Camarena was taken. He was *actually at the house and present while Kiki was tortured and interrogated.* And he was there when he was ultimately killed. He told me what exactly happened on that day. It would be the first and only time the DEA would hear an account of the events from someone who was an eyewitness to it all.

Chapter 22

The Killing House

On the morning of Thursday, February 7, 1985, a group of *pistoleros*, all of whom worked for members of the Guadalajara Cartel, gathered together at 881 Lope de Vega, a big hacienda in Guadalajara owned by Zuno. He was a *majore narco-politico*, one who had both a strong connection to the legitimate power structure of Mexico (he was the brother-in-law of a former Mexican president) as well as intimate ties with the Guadalajara Cartel.

Quintero rented the hacienda from Zuno and on that day three of the major leaders of the Guadalajara Cartel were there: Quintero, Gallardo and Fonseca. These three men were personally invested in overseeing and conducting an audacious plan to kidnap a person in the middle of the day in the heart of Guadalajara City. They had hired about 80 *pistoleros* to help them pull it off.

The *pistoleros* were never told who the target was, only that he was a very important man. Given the secrecy of the task and the nervousness of their bosses, the *pistoleros* speculated among themselves that their subject would have to be an *American*. Where they had come from, kidnapping a Mexican would never be cause for such concern. The *pistoleros* mingled around the hacienda until about 1:30 p.m. when someone showed up announcing that he had just come from the U.S. Consulate. "Everybody hurry up! The lawman is getting ready to go out for lunch. We need to do it now!"

Though the person who made this announcement was never identified, he must have either had direct access to Kiki's schedule or known somebody who did because his information was correct: The lawman was just about to leave for lunch. He had made plans to meet his wife, Mika, at a nearby Chinese restaurant. The lawman's name was Kiki Camarena.

Five cars left the hacienda at 881 Lope de Vega and headed for the U.S. Consulate building in downtown Guadalajara. Inside the lead car were three DFS agents, one of Quintero's most trusted gunmen and the mysterious man from the consulate. The four other cars were filled with *pistoleros*. They would follow and park at each corner around the consulate. Their plan was to have Rene Lopez, who would later become my witness, and the DFS agents kidnap Kiki right there in front of the building as he left for lunch. If there was any resistance, the *pistoleros* would be ready to pounce. They were armed to the max with fully automatic weapons, thousands of rounds of ammunition and grenade launchers. They were also ordered to kill anyone who tried to stop or disrupt the kidnapping. Had this happened, it would have been a bloodbath.

It takes around 15 minutes to drive from the hacienda to the consulate, and when the five cars arrived, they pulled into their assigned positions and waited. Less than five minutes later, they spotted Kiki leaving the building and walking across the street toward his DEA undercover truck. The lead car with the DFS agents pulled up alongside him and one of the agents said, "Hey Kiki."

Kiki looked at them and said, "Hey, what's going on?"

The DFS agents stepped out of the car. "You need to come with us. The *comandante* wants to talk to you."

Kiki wasn't panicked. "Okay, but I need to notify my office first."

He started to reach for his radio handset, but before he could, one of the DFS agents stuck his gun into Kiki's ribs and said, "No radio, motherfucker. You're coming with us, now."

Kiki did not put up a fight, genuinely believing there must've been some kind of misunderstanding and that once he got to the DFS *comandante's* office, he'd clear it up, no problem. Whatever he was thinking, within seconds of him being dragged into the back of their car, he must have known there was something else in play, something far more sinister.

One of the agents made a radio call of his own: *"The doctor has seen the patient,"* he said, which was the abductors pre-arranged code for *"We have him."* They threw a jacket over Kiki's head and sped off.

It was a brazen kidnapping — on a busy street right in broad daylight. There were also dozens of witnesses, but they most likely assumed it was just someone being arrested. Sadly, someone being dragged off the streets by the DFS was nothing out of the ordinary.

Welcome to Guadalajara.

• • • • •

As soon as they reached the hacienda at 881 Lope de Vega, they pulled Kiki out of the car, stood him up and blindfolded him with medical gauze and tape. Then they walked him to the patio where Fonseca and Quintero were waiting with a Mexican army colonel. Quintero walked up to Kiki and looked at him with disgust. "Hello, motherfucker," he said, "This is the way I've always wanted you." And he slapped Kiki across the face, followed by a punch to his solar plexus.

Kiki sunk to his knees. He must have recognized Quintero's voice from various wiretaps because he said, "Rafa, I can do you more good alive than dead."

Quintero said, "I ain't no Rafa, motherfucker. Why are you saying I'm Quintero?" He kicked Kiki again before ordering the DFS agents to take him to the maid's quarters.

Think about that: *A drug lord giving orders to Mexican federal law enforcement officers about what to do with a kidnapped DEA agent.*

The DFS agents took Kiki into the maid's quarters of the hacienda. Once inside, they cut the cords off a set of Venetian blinds and used them to tie Kiki's hands behind his back. They tied his ankles together as well and told him to sit down on the bed.

At that point, the DFS agents told Quintero, Fonseca and Gallardo that they were going to tape-record the interrogation.

Then it began.

What was passed off as an "interrogation" was nothing short of the absolute brutalization of a human being. For hours and hours and hours, Kiki's abductors beat him mercilessly. They hit him with blows to his head. They kicked him in the stomach. They burned him with cigarettes. They pulled out chunks of hair from his head. On the tapes that would later be furnished to investigators, the sounds of Kiki's bones cracking can be heard as he cries out in pain. His cries were met with laughter and ridicule.

The Last Narc

Pistoleros like Lira had been accustomed to kidnappings while in the Guadalajara Cartel. But as he explained to me, there was something different about the kidnapping of Camarena. He had never seen his bosses concerned — over anything. There was an air of urgency about the abduction of the DEA agent. Everyone involved seemed to recognize the inherent danger of what they were doing. The danger was elevated when the Cuban, Max Gomez, showed up with a pair of Cuban bodyguards of his own. Lira had never seen his bosses defer to anyone. Ever. But when the Cuban showed up, they all fell into line. The Cuban also interrogated Kiki. Lira said that his manner of interrogation suggested he was "training" the DFS and cartel members on how to do it properly. He used water on the DEA agent, explaining the method of "waterboarding," which Lira had never seen. He said the Cuban asked him about other things like the camp at Veracruz and who else knew about it. Max Gomez and his Cuban bodyguards didn't stay long, leaving quite suddenly as if they had gotten what they came for. While Lira didn't like Max Gomez or his bodyguards, they did bring a semblance of order to the chaos. Once they left, Quintero was back in charge and things seemed to devolve into brutal madness again, with Kiki being beaten well into the night.

· · · · ·

On the second day, February 8th, the interrogators grew even more sadistic. They took turns smashing Kiki in the face with the butts of their AK-47s until they knocked out all of his teeth and dislocated his jaw. They opened their rifle cartridges and sprinkled the gun powder on him before lighting a fire so it would burn his neck and face. At one point during the torture, he begged for an honorable death. He pleaded with his torturers to put a bullet in his head. But the torturers would not honor his pleas. They stripped him down, broke off the handle of a broom and sodomized him.

Repeatedly.

Lira spoke of a revolving door of some of Mexico's most important *politicos* popping over to see the spectacle. Mexico's Defense Minister, General Arévalo Gardoqui, stopped by. A half-dozen of Mexican Federal Judicial Police's most decorated *comandantes* showed up. Even the cartel's fourth biggest drug lord, Juan Ramón Matta Ballesteros, flew in from Tegucigalpa, Honduras to personally witness some of the interrogation. Other notable participants were Manuel "Cochi Loco" Salcido Uzeta, as well as a young thug named Joaquín "El Chapo" Guzman.

By noon of day two, Kiki was near death. His blood painted the walls and floors of the maid's quarters. His ribs were broken. He bled from the rectum. He could barely breath. And the relentless blows to his head left him in a concussed, incoherent state. He didn't even know where he was. Finally, after hours of the most masochistic torture imaginable, Kiki gave up the one and only name interrogators would ever get from him. It was the name of the pilot who'd supposedly flown him and other DEA agents over the marijuana fields the cartel owned at Rancho Búfalo. The pilot's name was Alfredo Zavala. Within moments Gallardo dispatched a group of his men, including El Chapo, with orders to kidnap the pilot. They did so without haste, abducting him at gunpoint from a hangar where he worked at the Guadalajara Airport. They brought him back to the killing house where he too was beaten without mercy.

As the second day gave way to night, and after several hours of more burning, more beating, more visitors, Kiki began to lose consciousness, fading in and out for long periods of time. This was problematic for cartel leaders. For all the hours spent beating and torturing him, they had still gleaned very little information. He had given them no names. No other agents who worked in Guadalajara, and no informants used by the DEA. And he had given them very little information on the Rancho Búfalo marijuana fields they were so obsessed with. He had given them next to nothing. *And now he was dying?*

Things only got worse.

Fonseca, the boss of bosses, had not been actively involved in Kiki's interrogation. He had ordered the abduction, but once he saw the agent captive, he returned to his home and left the interrogation to Quintero and the DFS agents. Any information that came from Kiki was immediately relayed to him via his men. However, when he returned to Lope de Vega the next day and saw Kiki's bloodied and lifeless body, he was mortified. It was alleged that Quintero defended his actions and the pair nearly came to blows. But cooler heads prevailed and Fonseca ordered they call a doctor with DFS credentials, a man by the name of Humberto Álvarez Macháin.

When Dr. Macháin arrived at the scene, Quintero told him, "This son of a bitch is dying on us. We need you to keep him awake." The doctor began injecting lidocaine directly into Kiki's heart. Lidocaine causes the heart to fibrillate faster, which pumps blood back to the brain, making even a severely injured person regain consciousness for short periods of time. Dr. Macháin injected just enough lidocaine for Kiki to be interrogated for a few more minutes before he passed out again. But this method didn't last long. Kiki had lost too much blood. His head was swollen and his face disfigured from all the beating. After one last fruitless injection, Dr. Machaín advised Quintero that if they did not get Kiki to the hospital, he was going to die. Quintero would have none of it.

"Fuck him!" he snapped at the doctor. "Let him die! Or make him talk!"

Dr. Machaín attempted one final technique to resuscitate Kiki. He put a plastic laundry bag over his head in the hopes that the lack of oxygen would be too torturous for him to endure. It didn't work. It then became obvious to all: Kiki was on his way out. Dr. Machaín turned to Quintero and said, "There's no saving him. This man is about to die."

Quintero thought about this for less than a second. "Fine. Bury him." And they called *los dormidos*. The sleepers.

The sleepers arrived at the killing house, picked up Kiki and threw him into the trunk of a car. One of the *dormidos* saw that Kiki was still gasping for breath, so he grabbed a piece of rebar and stuck it through Kiki's skull.

He was 37 years old.

Before they departed, one of the *pistoleros* said, "Hey, what about the pilot?"

"Bury him as well," Quintero ordered.

They put Zavala in the trunk of a second car and drove out to Primavera Park where they dug a hole and buried Kiki and the pilot in the same grave. Zavala was still alive when they buried him.

Chapter 23

Aguas Warning

With knowledge of the event now coming from firsthand witnesses, I continued debriefing the other informants. Some of them would later become witnesses. Questioned separately, all verified the information that Ramon Lira had so courageously shared. I now believed without a doubt that Felix Rodriguez of the CIA was there. To prove this, I put together a line-up of mug shots of Cubans known to work for the CIA, which I presented to my firsthand witnesses. Every single one of them pointed to the same man and said, "*That guy. That's Max Gomez. That Cuban motherfucker was there.*"

That Cuban motherfucker, the one they identified as the man inside the hacienda at 881 Lope de Vega in Guadalajara, was none other than Felix Rodriguez.

• • • • •

The *pistoleros* didn't know about Felix Rodriguez, but I sure as hell did. I knew he was a longtime CIA operative involved in the Bay of Pigs and Watergate. I also knew that he had been one of the leaders in the apprehension and killing of Che Guevara in 1967 in

Bolivia. Rodriguez was the one who'd cut off Guevara's hands with a hack saw and shipped them back to the CIA and FBI to prove the man he'd helped track down and kill was in fact Che Guevara. The most recent information I knew about Rodriguez was that he was involved with CIA operations in Nicaragua. I immediately wanted to know: *What the fuck was a Cuban CIA operative last seen in Nicaragua doing Contra shit? What was this guy doing in Guadalajara, hanging around in a hacienda with a bunch of drug lords while a DEA agent was being tortured to death?*

I ran Rodriguez's name through the DEA's computer database called Narcotics and Dangerous Drugs Information System, or NADDIS, which included every report any DEA agent in the world had filed on a suspected drug operation or narcotics trafficker. The name Felix Rodriguez lit up NADDIS like a Christmas tree. There were many different reports from investigations scattered all over the world that included DEA intelligence on his suspicious activities. But up to that point no one had put the pieces together.

For starters, I learned through NADDIS that in 1984 one of Rodriguez's business partners, Gerard Latchinian, had been arrested with $10 million's worth of cocaine. At the time of this arrest, Rodriguez was using the services of one of the Medellín Cartel's chief accountants, Ramon Milian, to launder cash from a dozen Miami companies for the Contras. I also learned that in 1985, a CIA engineer and pilot named Terry Reed had fingered Rodriguez for personally overseeing the shipment of cocaine through a CIA manufacturing front company named Machinery International, which was headquartered in Guadalajara and manufactured weapons for the Contras. Reed also reported that Rodriguez was using CIA contract pilot Barry Seal to smuggle tons of cocaine from Colombia into a secret U.S. military airbase in Mena, Arkansas maintained by the CIA where Contra pilots were being trained in the early to mid-1980s. Another NADDIS report mentioned that Rodriguez was suspected of storing cocaine in airplane hangars controlled by the CIA at the Ilopango Airport in El Salvador. Yet another report indicated that Rodriguez was suspected of running cocaine from Mexico into that same Mena, Arkansas air base.

    I investigated Rodriguez deeper and learned that he and an associate, Luis Posada Carriles, were involved in blowing up Cubana Flight 455, which was carrying Cuba's Olympic fencing team from Venezuela to Cuba on October 6, 1976, killing 73 people. Rodriguez then hired Carriles to assist him in a Contra resupply operation after Carriles' escape from a Venezuelan prison where he'd been serving time for blowing up the plane. I found out that Rodriguez had been deeply involved in the CIA's notorious Operation Phoenix campaign of interrogations, torture and assassinations in Southeast Asia during the Vietnam War. There were also DEA reports that showed Rodriguez was funneling drug monies to the Nicaraguan Contras through Ramon Milian. This money was being used for that Contra resupply operation in Nicaragua. As I tried to make sense of this, something in my past would provide clarity.

• • • • •

    It was daybreak on Monday, October 27, 1986 and I was still working in L.A. Three days before, I'd attended a briefing of more than 100 law enforcement agents from the FBI, DEA and Los

Angeles Sheriff's Department. By this time, America was in the middle of a massive drug crisis. It seemed as if overnight, cocaine was flooding cities all over the country, including South Central Los Angeles where the Bloods and Crips were cooking "crack," the super-addictive, smokable form of cocaine that cost just a few dollars a hit. A DEA Special Agent named Tom Schrettner had pieced together intelligence about a new drug ring supplying the cocaine, importing hundreds of kilos through Mexico every month. The ring was said to be run by a man named Oscar Danilo Blandón, the head of agricultural imports in the government of the former Nicaraguan dictator Anastasio Somoza.

At the briefing, Sergeant Tom Gordon of the L.A. Sheriff's Department narcotics strike force explained that his department had reliable information that Blandón's crew had stash houses all over the Los Angeles area and that the locations had been identified. Furthermore, Blandón was sending millions of dollars in cash to Florida where it was being laundered and funneled to the Contra rebel army in Nicaragua.

I had a basic knowledge of who the Contras were. I knew they were anti-communist, which meant, in my book, that they were the good guys. I didn't understand, nor did the American public, that the Contras were basically an extension of the CIA. Now that I was investigating Kiki's murder and had discovered a more nefarious undertow to the case, it occurred to me that there was something fishy about a former Nicaraguan government official suddenly showing up in L.A. and selling hundreds of kilos of cocaine, the proceeds of which were going to a CIA-organized guerrilla army.

Aside from not understanding this, I did not care. I was a special agent for the DEA. I did my job and never paid much attention to politics. I was a gunslinger. All I heard was, *There's a new big-time coke dealer in town, and we're going to bust 14 of his stash houses in a multi-agency operation.*

That was good enough for me.

The task force put me in charge of leading the entry team at one of the stash houses located in the city of Montclair, California. One of the guys on my team was this really gung-ho L.A. Sheriff's Deputy, kind of a surfer kid. We had surveillance on the house that showed it had a pretty heavy security front door. When we got ready to hit the house, I assigned this young deputy to connect a metal tow hook to the security grate on the back door of the place, then run a metal tow chain from the hook to his sheriff's department jeep.

According to our plan, unless I gave him a signal right away that we'd made entry through the front door, he would rev up that jeep and rip the back door off the house so the rear entry team could make the breach. And he was really eager, man. He was good to go. Just after dawn on October 27, 1986, our task force hit all 14 of Blandón's stash houses, which were spread out all over L.A. County — and we hit them simultaneously.

Then shit got very weird very fast.

I was used to raiding stash houses at dawn. Typically, dopers party or weigh and package product late into the night, so they're by nature late risers. You hit their spot when the sun is barely up because you expect them to be asleep. You sure as hell don't expect them to answer the door. As soon as I knocked and shouted, "DEA! Search Warrant!" this Nicaraguan guy, not Blandón but one of his partners, opened the door and was just as pleasant as can be. He was wide-awake, showered, dressed and friendly. He said, "Good morning officers, good morning. We've been expecting you. Please, please, come in. Would you like some coffee?"

What?

A couple of minutes later, we started getting reports on the radio from the raid teams at the other 13 locations, and it was the same story over and over again. The people inside were awake and dressed and offering them coffee. Hell, at some of the places they even had doughnuts.

And no one was finding any coke.

We had reliable information that a lot of kilos were in these houses, but not on that morning. Though we searched and searched, there was no coke to be found in any of them.

At the house my team went into, we did find a safe. When I asked the guy who'd answered the door to open it, he did so, a little reluctantly. Inside was a money ledger that looked like a record of cocaine sales. The numbers of units matched up with the prices in such a way that it seemed to me like a ledger recording kilos sold for less than average street value, but still a lot. Unfortunately, it was nothing we could arrest him for.

The other 13 houses were all just as clean, except the search teams in a few of them found Contra propaganda and recruitment fliers.

· · · · ·

The curious relationship between the CIA, the Guadalajara Cartel and the Nicaraguan Contras was now very clear to me. I went back into my notes from very early in my investigation when I learned that the pilot who had flown Quintero out of Mexico after

Kiki's murder was a man named Warner Lutz. Lutz was a well-known contract pilot who the CIA had worked with on many occasions. I then learned that the plane Lutz had used for that flight out of Mexico was a SETCO Falcon Jet. Yes, the same line of jets owned by drug lord Juan Ramon Matta Ballesteros.

It was around this time that I detected strange sounds on my home telephone. The sounds were familiar to me — sounds omitted by pen registers, which are used when phones are being wiretapped. I had my home phone checked by the DEA's Tec Unit who ran a laser on my line and discovered that my line was indeed being tapped! We checked the telephone lines at the DEA Los Angeles Field Division and discovered that the lines assigned to the Leyenda Unit were also being intercepted.

Un-fucking-believable.

Equally unbelievable was that nobody among the higher-ups at the administration even seemed to give a damn. As if, *"Oh, well. Nothing to see here..."*

Having exhausted my investigation, I gathered all the evidence I had concerning everything and everyone: Felix Rodriguez, Larry Harrison, the cartel's "friend from the DEA," connections between the CIA and DFS — all the evidence I had obtained during Operation Leyenda. This included audio recordings, polygraph results and evidence from Assistant United States Attorney Susan Bryant-Deason. I turned it in to the DEA's Office of Professional Responsibility. It would be their job to forward all that evidence to the Office of the Inspector General, which, unlike the DEA, had the authority to investigate federal intelligence agencies for illegal wrongdoing. My superiors promised me that OPR would take it from there.

They didn't. A week turned into a month, and then another, and it became very clear to me that nothing would ever come of it. When I pressed my superiors, I was told that I could not to go down that road, that I should not even think about going after Felix Rodriguez or a fellow DEA agent. I was told to limit my investigations to the Mexican cartel figures — and that's it.

Nobody from the Office of Professional Responsibility would ever get back to me. *And all that evidence I had gathered?* It was like it disappeared into a big black hole.

Chapter 24

Arrest of a Vicious Sicario

It was ironic that while my CIA-centric investigation of Kiki's murder had come into focus, I could not see clearly that my career was beginning to fray. I had known what it was like to be a rising star at the DEA. I had been part of some of the biggest busts in the agency's history. I had been front and center at legendary shootouts. I had been decorated and promoted and slapped on the back. But that was no longer the case. Because I am an undercover, at my very core I am acute to surroundings and the perceptions of others. As my investigation carried on, I could tell that I was no longer an agent who others liked to joke with around the water cooler or slap hands with in the hall as we passed one another. I could hear their hushed whispers when I walked by and I could feel the weight of their suspicious stares. In their minds, I had wondered off the DEA reservation. I was no longer viewed as a "company man." I was now being looked upon as a "traitor."

Despite my career's downward spiral, I managed to land one final blow in the investigation when I made a key arrest of one of the cartel's killers. He had been wandering around Mexico free as a bird until I caught up with him. He was a killer known as "El Güeron," who, along with Juan Jose Bernabe Ramirez, was responsible for the murder of four Jehovah's Witnesses just months before Kiki's. My witnesses reported that the two men had repeatedly raped the women until they bled before gruesomely killing them. The pair were also said to be involved in Kiki's kidnapping and murder, though I wasn't sure. All I know is that as I listened to what the witnesses told me, I was consumed once again by anger and a desire for revenge.

El Güeron's real name was Jorge Fonseca Carrillo. Note his last name, "Fonseca." Yes, he was also the half-brother of drug lord Ernesto Fonseca Carrillo and owned the ranch where the Jehovah's Witnesses were tortured and killed. I was informed that Bernabe, a former Jalisco state police officer and trusted executioner for Fonseca and Quintero, resided in Guadalajara and continued to provide service as a gun-for-hire to the cartel.

I immediately went about setting up a sting operation against these two vicious sexual deviants and asked my cadre of informants if they had a way to get close to these guys. None of them thought they could get close enough to El Güeron. However, former DFS *comandante* Federico Castel del Oro informed me that he knew Bernabe quite well and thought he could approach him with a ruse to bring him to the United States. I arranged for Castel del Oro's travel to Guadalajara. In short order he called me from Mexico and told me that Bernabe had agreed to travel to Los Angeles with him, believing a major drug dealer from California needed his services.

A day after Castel del Oro arrived in Los Angeles with Bernabe, I was introduced to him as major drug dealer Manuel Lizarraga, a large scale cocaine distributor to the Hollywood elite. During the undercover meeting, I informed Bernabe that I was constantly being harassed and investigated by a U.S. customs agent who I wanted eliminated. He told me that for the right amount of money he could have that customs agent disappeared. He said he had killed many people in Mexico for the Guadalajara Cartel, including cops. He had no qualms about killing a law enforcement official. He offered to kill the customs agent for the price of $100,000 — $50,000 up front and the balance to be paid upon the death the agent.

I agreed to pay that amount of money, but I also informed him that I needed to be sure he was the vicious killer he was claiming to be. I pressed him to tell me what officials he had killed for the cartel. His answer was that I should ask Castel del Oro, bragging, "He knows I have killed a lot of people for the cartel in Mexico."

I asked him if he knew Fonseca and Quintero. Bernabe said he had worked as a hired gun for both.

"Check me out, you'll see I'm for real."

I said I would, though I didn't need to. He was real. *A real piece of shit.*

Our undercover meeting took place at a downtown Los Angeles hotel and was recorded using a Kele-unit (a hidden transmitter) taped to my chest underneath my clothes. By the time the meeting ended, I had promised to supply Bernabe with the name and picture of the U.S. customs agent I wanted him to kill. But I didn't get the one thing I'd been after: incriminating evidence that he had been involved in the murder of Kiki Camarena.

About a month later, Bernabe returned to the L.A. area and asked me to meet with him again. During this second undercover meeting, he pressed me to provide him with the name, address and photograph of the U.S. customs official. He also wanted me to deliver the $50,000 front money so that he could complete the execution during this same visit to the United States.

I decided to play a cat and mouse game for a while, so I told him what I had told him before: that I wasn't going to give him any money until I was convinced he was the experienced executioner he claimed to be. I needed to get him to admit on tape that he had been involved in Kiki's murder, and it had to come out of him without being directly solicited. But again, all I could get out of him was, "Check me out. Everybody in the know in Mexico knows I am the most prolific executioner the cartel has ever had. I will kill anyone, at any place, at any time for the right amount of money."

I could tell that Bernabe was indeed the psychopath he claimed to be. I know this isn't scientific. But I knew a killer when I saw one. And I could see death in his eyes. He had a penetrating gaze and a diabolical laugh. Not since driving with Fragoso down in Douglas had I been in the presence of such evil. The second meeting ended without him admitting his involvement in Kiki's murder, or in the rapes and murders of the Jehovah's Witnesses.

Two weeks later, Bernabe returned to the United States and once again asked to meet with me. This time DEA Special Agent Delbert Salazar accompanied me as an added undercover agent. We met at the bar of the El Torito restaurant in Covina, California. During the meeting Bernabe repeated his request that I front him the $50,000 he needed to start planning the custom agent's murder. Again I told him that I was not willing to deliver that kind of money unless I was absolutely convinced he was capable of killing a law enforcement officer. This time he finally said it. "Listen, I've killed many cops for the cartel in Mexico, and I was particularly involved in killing an American federal agent in Mexico."

Playing dumb, I asked, "What American agent?"

"You know who. That asshole we picked up for Quintero."

I backed up a little and kept ordering drinks. I didn't want him to freeze on me. I needed to keep him calm and keep him talking into the concealed microphone I wore under my shirt. I shifted the conversation and after ten minutes of talking about nothing — which seemed like an eternity — I returned to the topic of Kiki's murder. "What American federal agent did Quintero order you to kidnap?"

"Camarena. His murder's been all over the news for years."

The door was open now and it was up to me to collect as much evidence as possible on this asshole's involvement. I wanted to ask him a million questions. To calm myself down, I ordered another round of drinks.

Feeling the warmth of the 1800 tequila double shot, I said, "So you're telling me you were involved in killing that DEA asshole that cost Quintero those big marijuana fields at El Búfalo?"

"Yes, I was," he replied with a horrible grin.

My first instinct was to grab my gun and shoot this prick in the face to wipe out that stupid grin forever. My second instinct was to arrest him on the spot. He had just confessed on tape to his involvement in Kiki's murder. But I had to control myself. I remembered the admonition from Assistant United States Attorney John Carlton: "Hector, please take your time with this guy, and get as much evidence as you can on tape. The more involvement he admits to, the stronger the case we'll have against him at trial."

I ordered another round and chased another double shot of tequila with a full can of Pacifico. Then I asked Bernabe, "Did you interrogate that asshole?"

He assured me that he had.

"Did he mention my name?"

"No, he did not. He never mentioned you."

I asked him to describe what Camarena looked like the last time he saw him. He told me he was very swollen from the severe beating he had endured and that the man was barely alive when he last laid eyes on him. I could not take anymore. I stood up, grabbed my badge with my left hand, grabbed my gun with my right hand and aimed directly into his face.

"U.S. Drug Enforcement. You are under arrest for murder."

When surveillance DEA agents saw me making the arrest, they all moved in waving guns and credentials and yelling at the other people in the bar.

"Everybody remain calm! We are U.S. government agents effecting an arrest!"

The agents grabbed Bernabe and placed him face down on the ground where he was searched and handcuffed. I picked him up, grabbed him by the wrists and walked him out of the bar. As we were walking out with the prisoner, the patrons in the bar started chanting, "U.S.A.!... U.S.A.!....U.S.A.!"

It felt great to be an American. Yes, it did. And it was a good day for the good guys.

· · · · ·

Months later, Bernabe was tried for Camarena's murder in the U.S. Central District Court in Los Angeles. I testified at length about my undercover meetings with him. The prosecutor played the undercover recordings of Bernabe assuring me that he had participated in the abduction, torture and murder of Kiki Camarena.

The court took a short recess during my cross-examination and I was feeling good — until Assistant U.S. Attorneys Manny Medrano and John Carlton told me that the defense was asking the judge permission to present new evidence that could possibly have Bernabe's recorded undercover admissions thrown out of court. I had known about these kind of last minute defense tactics, and usually they were just a desperate attempt by the defense team. Most of the time the judge in the case would rule them inadmissible.

But upon resuming testimony, we were all shocked when we learned that the judge had granted their request. *And what was this last minute piece of key evidence?* The bar tab for the drinks we had consumed during the last undercover meeting at the El Torito bar and grill.

It was for over $300.

• • • • •

"Agent Berrellez," the defense counsel began. "What exactly was my client drinking during the undercover meeting?"

"He was drinking Corona beers and shots of Hornitos Tequila," I replied.

"And what were you drinking?"

"I was drinking Pacifico beers and shots of Cuervo Gold 1800 tequila."

"And what was Agent Delbert Salazar drinking?"

"He was drinking Budweiser." And then looking straight at the jurors, I added, *"Bud Light,"* to which they all started laughing.

When things quieted, the defense counsel continued. "If the bar tab is correct, would you agree that you had my client consume 15 beers and 15 shots of tequila during the undercover meeting?"

I replied, "If that is what is on the bar tab then that amount is correct."

With that, he went in for the kill.

"In other words, you got my client totally drunk!" he snapped. "Because it was the only way to get him to say things he might not have said had he been sober!"

I stayed cool before I said, "I can't say for sure, sir. I don't know what his tolerance for alcohol is."

"And what about you?" he scoffed.

"What about me?"

"You consumed 15 Pacifico beers and 18 shots of tequila? Weren't you drunk?"

"Well, no sir. I was tipsy at times, but I felt I was always in control of the conversation and never lost track of the investigative strategy. Sometimes we are required to consume alcohol as part of our undercover roles."

The attorney gave a smug glance over to the jurors as if to imply I was full of shit and he was done with me.

But the ploy didn't work. The jury didn't buy it. They convicted Bernabe of murder and sentenced him to life plus ten years in federal prison on charges related to Kiki's murder.

Chapter 25

Betrayal

The first clue that I was about to be thrown to the wolves surfaced in January 1993, not long after Jack Lawn retired. (Lawn was the administrator of the DEA who personally authorized me to conduct the kidnapping operations in Mexico, including the kidnapping of Dr. Machaín.) After Lawn retired, the George H. W. Bush administration named Terrence "Terry" Burke the acting administrator of the DEA. Terry Burke was not a "home grown" DEA agent. Prior to coming to the DEA, he was a CIA intelligence officer stationed in the Middle East. In fact, Burke had been brought into the DEA to spy on the agency under a longstanding effort called Operation Twofold in which 200 former CIA officers were absorbed into the DEA starting in the 1970s. Most of these operatives were placed in foreign DEA offices. They were typically Anglo paramilitary officers whose careers had stalled due to the gradual reduction of CIA forces in Vietnam and Laos.

A couple of weeks after Burke's appointment, I was summoned to the office of the Special Agent in Charge in Los Angeles. Waiting for me were two investigators from the Office of Professional Responsibility, the DEA's equivalent of internal affairs — the same office that I'd been promised would forward my evidence of CIA wrongdoing in Kiki's murder to the Office of the

Inspector General. The investigators informed me they were there to question me for their investigation into the kidnapping of Dr. Macháin, which had suddenly, two years after the actual rendition took place, become an international incident.

As explained previously, the rendition of Dr. Macháin was not shared with then U.S. Ambassador to Mexico Charles Pilliod. Nor was it shared with DEA Country Attaché Ralph Saucedo. Once the Mexican media learned of the abduction, fury spread throughout the nation and rocked the halls of the Mexican government. As chief architect of the rendition, I knew that most of the attribution for the kidnapping would fall upon me. I had already accepted that. What I didn't know was that the entire attribution would be shoveled upon me. Now it was becoming crystal clear.

The good doctor Macháin, despite vigorous protests from the Mexican government, was tried in United States District Court in Los Angeles, but his defense did an outstanding job diverting the doctor's guilt, focusing instead on the legality of the arrest. His trial would result in an acquittal. That wasn't good enough for the Mexico's president, Carlos Salinas de Gortari, who demanded my immediate arrest and extradition from the United States. I had never been concerned about this demand because my involvement was the result of a direct order from the administrator of the DEA. That was until I walked from the SAC's office to a DEA interrogation room, a room I'd used often to interrogate suspects. Now I was the one about to be interrogated by investigators from my own agency. The OPR guys informed me that I was officially under criminal investigation and advised me of my constitutional Miranda rights, which of course I knew very well and could recite word-for-word.

When they asked if I'd talk to them without a defense attorney present, I told the truth: "I have nothing to hide." They asked me to sign a statement that I had been advised of my rights and was choosing to speak to them without a lawyer present. I signed it. They began the interrogation by asking me if I was personally responsible for kidnapping Dr. Macháin.

"Yep," I said.

Next they asked me if I thought I'd done anything wrong in regards to the kidnapping. I misunderstood their question. I thought they were asking me if I'd done anything wrong in terms of how I'd carried out the operation: the logistics, the blow-by-blow of how our team had abducted him. I thought that since the order to carry out the kidnapping had come from the very top, I was protected.

So I replied, "Well, I probably made some mistakes, because I'd never kidnapped anyone before. But for a first-time kidnapper, I think I did okay. We got Dr. Macháin into the United States and no one got hurt."

"Okay, how was this operation conducted?"

I explained to them in detail how I'd been ordered by the administrator of the DEA to arrange the kidnapping of Dr. Macháin. That I'd never been trained in kidnapping and I had never kidnapped anyone before, so I just used my imagination: I began by buying cops in Mexico, the same way criminals buy cops in Mexico. Essentially, that I had paid a group of corrupt police officers in Mexico to carry out the kidnapping of the doctor. They took careful notes. I gave up everything about how it had been done. How the money was paid, who it was paid to, everything.

Throughout the questioning, OPR Inspector Matthew Mahr went out of his way to badger me, intimidate me and humiliate me by using patronizing language. He kept referring to me as *"Amigo,"* and after every question he would ask me, *"Comprende señor?"* Except that he pronounced it *"seeenyor"* in exaggerated, sarcastic fashion, as if I were some caricature of a sleepy Mexican. Twice I informed him that I was born in America and that I was a university graduate who spoke English fluently, but he kept up with his *"Comprende seeenyor"* bullshit.

After the interview was concluded and they left, I called some friends of mine at DEA headquarters in Washington, D.C. and asked, "Why in the hell am I being criminally investigated for carrying out orders from the administrator of the DEA?" They told me that Acting Administrator Terry Burke was entertaining the idea of surrendering me to the FBI to be arrested and extradited to Mexico to face prosecution for the kidnapping of Dr. Machaín. Well, that was fucking nice. One administrator of the DEA orders me to kidnap the doctor and now the acting administrator who replaces him is thinking about arresting me and handing me over to the Mexican government. If that happened, the best-case scenario was that I'd rot in a Mexican prison. The more likely scenario was that I'd face the same fate as Kiki Camarena. I would be kidnapped. Tortured. And executed.

It was the ultimate betrayal.

So, at this point in my life, the country of Mexico wanted me extradited so I could spend the rest of my life in jail if I was lucky. I had been green-lit by the Guadalajara Cartel for death. My own agency hated me. And oh, the CIA wanted me out of the picture too.

I was in deep shit. And this time there would be no stick hidden in the bushes to save me.

· · · · ·

The betrayal continued when President Bill Clinton held a press conference in which he said the operation to kidnap Dr. Macha*í*n had been conducted by a "rogue agent." Clinton added, "The thought of a DEA agent kidnapping a Mexican citizen makes me want to vomit."

The *Washington Post* ran an article quoting DEA Press Information Officer Frank Shultz as stating, "The kidnapping of the doctor was carried out by a rogue renegade agent, Hector Berrellez, without headquarters' knowledge nor authorization."

On its face, this was absurd. As if I just woke up one morning and said to myself, *You know what? Fuck it. I'm just going to kidnap this rich and politically connected doctor in Mexico all on my own to avenge Kiki Camarena whether the DEA likes it or not, consequences be damned.*

I could have defended myself by exposing the truth, but I didn't. *Why?* Because I'd been sworn to secrecy. And though I had been betrayed, I was still loyal — even after they disowned me in the media. I could have gone public and reported the CIA for illegally wiretapping my home phone as well as the phones of all the Operation Leyenda agents working under my supervision. We had found their eavesdropping equipment within the DEA Los Angeles Field Division's electrical utility room, and the security director of the phone company confirmed to us that the CIA planted bugs on our office phones. I thought I was doing my patriotic duty by taking the fall. I was still idealistic. Maybe even a little stupid. Only now do I have clarity.

Within the DEA, I began to be treated as persona non grata. An example of this came just after Jack Lawn retired. The former administrator had, without my knowledge, put through the paperwork to honor me with an award. The award itself, the plaque, was sent to the office of the SAC of the Los Angeles Division of the DEA where I was stationed. He was a new SAC named Robert Bender.

One day, Bender told my supervisor, Mike Holm, "Tell Hector Berrellez to come up to my office and you come up with him."

When we walked in, Bender barely even acknowledged me before saying, "Hey, somebody forgot to give you this." He handed me the plaque. Didn't shake my hand, didn't say "Congratulations." It was just, *"Here's a piece of wood and metal with your name on it that somebody forgot to give you. Now get out of my office."* There was no public presentation. No ceremony. Nobody else in the DEA knew I received that award. That's how I was treated. Like I was just a fuck-up. I took the award and walked out, not saying another word to anyone. Not until I got back to my desk did I look at it. It was the highest award the DEA could bestow upon its agents. An award usually given out during expensive banquets and gushing accolades. It was the DEA Administrator's Award.

· · · · ·

The foul treatment I endured at the hands of the agency I once loved continued under the permanent administrator who replaced Terry Burke. This man's name was Tom Constantine. He treated me like shit. He glared at me around DEA headquarters. He never gave me the slightest bit of respect. He didn't bother speaking to me. I used to say, "Good morning, Mr. Administrator," and Constantine wouldn't even acknowledge my existence. He made it known that he detested me.

Just as Terry Burke was a surrogate of the CIA, Tom Constantine was a surrogate of the FBI. Constantine was a New York state police administrator for most of his career before he was named administrator of the DEA. He had zero experience with street narcotics investigations and zero experience with foreign investigations. He became the administrator of the DEA at a time when there was a big push from the Department of Justice to incorporate the DEA into the FBI, to basically make the DEA a drug unit of the FBI. The only reason it didn't happen was because the chiefs of police in local and state agencies in nearly every state in the country objected vehemently. They said, "Don't do this. We like the DEA the way it is. The DEA works with us in the streets. They're right there beside us when we kick down doors. The FBI does after-the-fact investigation. We catch the bank robbers and then the FBI swoops in and takes over the investigation. The DEA works the street with us, so no, we don't want the FBI taking over the DEA, thank you very much."

Eventually, the Department of Justice backed off the idea.

But Constantine's attitude was that DEA guys were a bunch of overpaid, trigger-happy cowboys. He said as much in his first meeting with all the agents in the Los Angeles field division. He said, "You feds..." He actually called us "feds" as if it was a dirty word, even though he's the director of a federal agency. He said, "You feds are overpaid."

The idea that we were overpaid was an insult. We had lost nine agents in the line of duty the year before he'd been in the administrator's office. Nine agents.

To Constantine, I personally represented everything he didn't like about the DEA, never mind the fact that the president of the United States had called me a renegade and a rogue agent. But all these guys — the Terry Burkes, the Constantines — they're all a bunch of kiss-asses. They're bean counters. All they think about is being politically correct. They couldn't handle working as street agents if they ever were street agents in the first place. And they wouldn't have lasted five minutes undercover. They're company men, and the corporation they work for is the U.S. government.

Meanwhile, OPR investigators continued trying to destroy me for another two years. They were looking to get me on anything they could. They investigated me for subornation of perjury and tried to pressure my informants to say that I had ordered them to lie or fabricate testimony. They investigated my interactions with prosecution witnesses, digging to see if they could make a case against me for fraternizing with them. They continually badgered the witnesses about whether I had underpaid any of them in an attempt to charge me with stealing money. It went on like this for the remainder of my career.

By the time I retired from the DEA, I could not wait to leave the agency I'd once loved. The minimum retirement age in the DEA is 50. If you're 50 years old, and you've put in 20 years of service, you can retire with benefits and a pension. If you prefer, you can stay until you're 57 and build up a much better pension. Most agents take the latter option. But I was being treated like a pariah. So on the first day I was eligible to retire, I put in my papers. The DEA didn't give me a going away party. There was no gold watch. No thank you. I just walked out the door. The day I started at the DEA, I walked in with no fanfare, because nobody knew me and I hadn't done shit for them. On my last day as a DEA agent, I walked out the door the same way.

As if nobody knew me and I'd never even been there.

Chapter 26

Death by Lead and Ink

People work their whole lives just to retire. I grew up in Arizona which has quite a few of retirees. During my youth, whether it was driving past a golf course or seeing an elderly couple walking around leisurely in the middle of the day — skin bronzed from being in the sun, an air of accomplishment on their faces, worry-free — it seemed like such an empty life. Golfing. Eating. Waiting around for your grandkids to visit. I always thought to myself, *never me*. I hated sitting still and I always loved what I did. I didn't think I would ever retire. Now, here I was, still only in my 50s and not a damn thing to do. I was miserable.

Most agents who leave federal law enforcement after two decades walk into a cushy job like "security consultation" or are given the opportunity to teach satellite courses in whatever they specialized during their years on the job. I could have been asked to teach undercover skills at the Academy. I could have educated young agents on the nature and history of the drug cartels. I could have even done law lectures on "extra-territorial rendition," a subject which I had quite intimate knowledge of. But none of these "glamour" jobs would come my way. The only "post DEA" opportunity I got was training cops in Panama on how to properly conduct and utilize polygraph tests. Don't get me wrong, it was work and it kept me sane. But it was like sending a 5-star chef to flip burgers at McDonald's.

In an earlier chapter of this book, I mentioned the dangers of being a DEA agent. The physical dangers of the job are well-documented. But there was an equally dangerous aspect to the job which I called a "moral" danger. As a working field agent, almost every deadly sin is at your fingertips in nearly every case. Greed can creep in when making a bust consisting of tens of millions of dollars and nobody would ever be the wiser if some of it went missing. When working around drugs and money, some of the most beautiful women in the world fall into your orbit, causing lust to spark up. *Why not cheat on your partner? They'll never find out.* If you are good at what you do, you will find yourself in the presence of pure evil, like I had with people like Fragoso and Bernabe. There were moments that took every fiber of my being to fight back the wrath I wanted to inflict. All I would have had to do was draw my gun, blast away and write in the report, *"he made a move for me."* But the physical and moral dangers of the job dissipate with retirement. The closest I would come to physical danger after I left was riding my horses. And the only moral dilemmas that would cross my path were whether to share with my wife if I had snuck a cigarette after quitting or "forgetting" to run an errand that I had promised. There was one last type of danger that I would encounter during my retirement that nobody had ever told me about. It was an *emotional danger*. Of all the dangers I had ever experienced as an agent, the greatest, most unpredictable and painful one was emotional. Especially when that emotion is grief.

Until now, I haven't written much of my family. Because I had worked for much of my career as an undercover and in some of the most dangerous places on the planet, I had always been fiercely protective of them. I had always been proud of the fact that I had, for the most part, shielded them from my ugly world. But the painful truth is my family needed more than just my protection. They needed my *presence*. In that department, I was a miserable failure. I wasn't a doting husband who shared with his wife. I wasn't a dad who went to his kids' parent-teacher conferences or to their games or anything, for that matter. I missed birthdays and holidays and just about every other memorable day a child is supposed to share with their father. Yes, I provided for all of them. And yes, I protected all of them. *But no, I was not present.* The person who bore the brunt of my failure was my oldest son, Pinky.

"Pinky" was not my first son's real name. He was named Hector. The first time I saw him was at the hospital maternity ward. I had sped there from work when I heard my wife had gone into labor. By the time I got to the hospital, he had already been born. I ran up to the floor where all the newborns were and I stared through the glass window at the 20 sleeping infants. I tried to figure out which baby was mine but I couldn't read their names. A nurse walked in and asked if she could help.

I said, "I'm looking for my new son but I don't know which one it is."

"Well, which one do you think it is?" she asked.

Then I figured, my wife was a beautiful light-skinned woman. And I was light skinned too. So I looked for the lightest-skinned baby there.

"I think he's that pink one over there."

And it was. My little Hector. Only we would never call him Hector. We could call him "Pinky" for the rest of his life.

Pinky grew up without me. Though he was a terrific athlete who was particularly great at baseball, I rarely saw him play. He would only show me his trophies when I was home and I would try to make a fuss over them. Pinky struggled in school and a troubled life would follow. He ended up having two children at a very young age with a woman who had problems of her own. And then he had two more kids with another woman, who left him for another man and took those two kids with her. Pinky fell into a deep depression.

My early retirement could have been a blessing at this time. I could have begun healing the wounds that the job inflicted on my family through years of my absence. I could have reconnected with my wife. I could have rebuilt my relationship with Pinky and my other son. But I was too bitter over the way my career ended. I was angry at the DEA. The federal government. The world. God. You name it. And I was too self-absorbed to see past my own misfortunes, most of which were the direct result of choices I had made during my life and career. Pinky could not say the same. Most of his troubles were because of me.

Pinky's pain and suffering came to a horrific end in an alcohol-induced state of depression. He pointed a gun to his own head. With his eldest boy watching, begging him to put the gun down, Pinky's final words to himself were, "Nobody loves me." Then he pulled the trigger. When I got home, my grandson still had the mist of his father's blood and brain all over his body.

· · · · ·

A lot of people wonder how a parent can survive something like the tragic suicide of their child. The truth is, *they don't.* I died

The Last Narc

that day. My marriage, which had been on the ropes anyway, died too. *Everything about me died.* My hope. My faith. My spirit. I had seen walking dead before. I had been in crack-houses and raided some of the most vile places on the planet. I've seen those hopeless souls who may be alive physically but look like they have departed this world. Their eyes are vacant. Their faces are devoid of any feeling or cognition. *That is who I became.* Those who could somehow penetrate my grief implored me to get help. See a priest. See a counselor. See a therapist. I would do none of it. Instead, I chose to see a doctor. Dr. Jose Cuervo.

I really don't know how I lived in the wake of Pinky's death. I got drunk the day he died and stayed drunk through the wake, through the funeral and through the ensuing weeks. I don't remember anything. All I can say is that not long after Pinky died, I found myself wandering Panama City, drunk off my ass.

I had an idea as to why I was in Panama City. I supposed that somewhere in the deepest recesses of my psyche, I thought it would be a good idea to forge on with my life and honor my commitment to teaching polygraph techniques at the country's military garrison. But I don't know how I got to Panama City or what I was even doing. I was wandering aimlessly around the Plaza Mayor. *Walking dead.* I do remember seeing fleeting images of vendors hawking goods, bars that wouldn't serve me and children who seemed to hide their faces when my gaze found theirs. I also remember staggering upon a very curious monument dedicated to Jules Dingler, a French engineer who tried to build the country's first canal back in 1884. Ill-planned, over-budgeted and attempted in the middle of what was the Yellow Fever epidemic, over 220,000 workers died. Just two years into the project, Dingler gave up. He shot his stallions, returned to France and died within a year. The spectacular failure would become known as "Dingler's Folly." As I stood in front of the memorial, I thought of what my own monument of failure might look like or say. *This memorial stone is dedicated to former DEA agent Hector Berrellez for totally fucking up his career. He was a shitty husband too. And oh, his eldest boy took his own life because he was never around as a father.*

After marinating in Dingler's failure, which seemed tame compared to mine, I staggered around the city some more until I came upon the part of town that I had been subconsciously seeking. It was the section that exists in every impoverished city in the world and looks like one of the rings of hell: strip clubs, saloons, pool rooms, massage parlors. Though it was still daylight, the area had an aura that made it appear as dark as 3:00 a.m. The denizens of these streets were not the bright-eyed tourists of the Plaza Mayor. They were night-crawlers, hiding until sunset. Hustlers, conspiring for the sins of that evening. In the middle of a particularly seamy run of bodegas was a small shop that looked like a slaughterhouse. Inside I saw about a half-dozen young men and one gal who were covered in blood. Hovering over each of them with a drill like an executioner was their "artist." It was a tattoo parlor. It looked altogether frightening, disgusting and painful. I had to get one.

I'm not a betting man, but I would wager that there is not a person reading these pages, Panamanian or not, who would ever consider getting a tattoo in Panama City a good idea. But for me, in that moment, it was perhaps the best idea I had ever come up with. I was still numb from Pinky's death. I had blurred the line of being hungover and drunk because I was both. I wanted the physical pain. I wanted the blood. I wanted the dirt. And I wanted to take a seat on one of the parlor's filthy chairs and sink deep into that world, all the way down to its soundless bottom. I wanted to drift so far below the depths of my misery that I would drown in its underbelly.

I took my seat in one of the chairs and a moment later one of the shop's tattooists appeared in front of me. He was a heavyset man and wore the skimpiest tee shirt I had ever seen on a person his size, exposing his own ink-riddled body. A cigarette dangled from one hand and in the other, the motorized contraption holding the needle that would create a virtually unremovable marking on my skin wherever I chose. The contraption was already painted in blood that wasn't my own. To make matters worse, my tattooist spoke neither English nor Spanish. Panamanians speak their own distinct dialect. It's basically the Pig Latin of the Hispanic speaking world. In short, neither one of us knew what the other was saying. To cut through the communication barrier, he handed me a small pad of paper and a pen and grunted something I interpreted as, "What the hell do you want?"

I had no idea. All I knew was that I wanted something for Pinky. So I scribbled down the words, *"Always in my heart, Pinky."*

I handed it to him and he studied it as if I had given him the structural specs for a cathedral. He took a massive drag from his cigarette, shrugged and looked at me one last time with an expression that said, "Where the hell do you want it?"

I pointed to my shoulder.

· · · · ·

I don't know how the next couple of weeks went as far as my teaching was concerned. I do recall that I was very fond of being called "doctor" by my students and fellow faculty at the garrison. My certification as an expert in the field of polygraph had somehow translated to "professor," which was further spoken as "doctor." I enjoyed it, but I'm sure they didn't enjoy that Dr. Berrellez was pretty much shit-faced from the moment he showed up. All I remember with absolute distinction is that not long after I got my tattoo, I began to experience some shoulder pain. I didn't really given it much thought. I figured it was supposed to be sore, because tattoos are painful, right? So whenever the pain kicked in, I drank some more. Soon enough the pain became very intense, so intense I thought I would give it a look. I hadn't even taken off the original bandage. When I saw it, my first thought was, *"Did I get a color tattoo?"* It was a massive patch of yellow mucus, green puss and bright red blood. I immediately went to see the garrison's doctor.

"Holy shit," he said. "This is bad."

"You might wanna work on your bedside manners, doc."

He gave me a disapproving glare. "When and where did you get it?"

"A couple of weeks ago. In Panama City."

"You got a tattoo in Panama City?" he asked, his disapproval now bordering on disgust. I nodded. *"Do you know how much AIDS there is in this country? Not to mention Hepatitis or any other number of infectious diseases?"*

My face went slack. *"You're telling me I could have AIDS?"*

"Of course you could, Dr. Berrellez. Sharing needles of any kind is one of the primary means of transmission."

I didn't think it was possible but I sank even lower. Here I was, a veteran of war. I had survived multiple gunfights. I had been green-lit by the world's most powerful drug cartel. And now, I was probably going to die from getting a fucking cheap tattoo while drunk in Panama City. I shook my head, now also disgusted with myself.

"You know, I'm not a doctor," I said.

"No shit."

• • • • •

The results for my AIDS test took a week to come back. I spent most of my time waiting for it as drunk as humanly possible. I had often heard the term "functioning alcoholics" but I never understood the concept. Not until I completed almost an entire course teaching young officers the vital skills that contribute to being a competent polygraph operator. I figured I must have been a functioning alcoholic. There was no other way to explain it. Either that or the teaching standards in Panamanian culture are tremendously low.

At some point during my waiting period, I seriously considered the ramifications of a positive test result. I had never feared death. During my life, I had made eye-contact with killers and heard bullets dropped into their chambers that were meant for me. I witnessed a man being thrown out of a plane. I drove a cab to a gun fight. I even arrested a fucking dog once. Guys like me did not die of AIDS because they got a bad tattoo when drunk. I decided with absolute certitude that if my test for AIDS came back positive, I would kill myself. Fuck you, Dingler, I thought to myself. *You want failure?* Hector Berrellez will give you failure on steroids with a crystal meth chaser. If I had AIDS, I was going to go see Pinky.

The test came back negative.

• • • • •

There are not Hallmark cards for every moment. If there were, I don't think a card from a loved one that said, *"Congratulations! You don't have AIDS!"* would have cheered me up. In fact, there was a small part of me that wished the test would have come back positive. Then I would've had an excuse to do what I really wanted to do. My truth was that I didn't want to live. I didn't want to carry on with my life. I hated where I was. I hated who I was. Nor could I summon the will to change either. The irony was that I still kept a holstered gun at my hip. It was one of the few perks I took with me into retirement: the license to openly carry a firearm. If I wanted to end it all, I had the power to do so at my fingertips. I lacked the courage and conviction to act on my desire, which made me hate myself even more.

There is a phrase in the equine world that has made its way into our lexicon: "put out to pasture." It is a reference to the practice of letting horses that are too old or too weak be freed from their stables to roam the pastures until they die. While the practice may be well-intentioned, the idiom's connotations are much more subtle and pernicious. And true. Horses put out to pasture often incur immediate problems. The sudden change in their diet can cause colic and metabolic syndrome, both of which bring about a cluster of clinical problems like obesity, diabetes and cardiovascular disease. Pastured horses will often lose their shoes as they try to navigate foreign landscapes. Many end up with founder, a painful inflammation of the hooves. Pastured horses tend to get more than a few scratches and scrapes. The exposure to sun results in the bleaching and dulling of their coat, which in turn thins out over time, diminishing its protection for the colder weather. For some horses, "put out to pasture" is just not viable. Many horses who are raised for trail or show have lost or forgotten their herd mentality. While a horse can be a wild animal, it is closer to a domesticated dog in its DNA. Many cannot live without the human interaction and love they were raised with. For those horses, being "put out to pasture" is a death sentence. This is exactly what I felt like. I could not function in the real world. The death of my career, my marriage and my oldest son had now put me out to a pasture of my own creation. It was a pasture of rolling hills of regret, acres and acres of bitterness and a stream of self-loathing that could never quench my thirst.

PART FIVE

RESURRECTION

If you live in the dark a long time and the sun comes out, you do not cross into it whistling. There's an initial uprush of relief at first, then a profound dislocation. The old assumptions about how the world works are buried. New ones aren't yet operational. There has been a death, but without a few days in hell, no resurrection is possible.

–Mary Karr, *Lit: A Memoir*

Chapter 27

Renacido
Reborn

In July of 2013, I was born again. Not in the spiritual sense, though that was still evolving, but rather a *physical sense*. At that time I was still mired in the mud of my past, but I could see shards of light breaking through the darkness. I was home alone as I usually was and tending to my horses when the call came.

"Hector," the voice on the other end of the phone said. "You're free. Your extradition request has expired."

I stood silent for a long moment. *Has it been over 20 years?* I wondered. *It couldn't be true.*

"Hector," the voice said. "Are you there?"

Finally, I spoke. "Yes, I'm here." Still uncertain, I asked, "What's that mean?"

"It means two things, my friend. One: You're old as shit. And two: Time to stop hiding and start living. You deserve it."

He hung up.

I stood there, still dazed by the news. I hadn't been hiding, exactly. But living on a ranch in rural San Bernardino County. I was certainly off grid. The caller was right. In my 70s now, I was "old as shit." But I had kept in terrific shape, still had a good head of hair and from a physical standpoint, I could not have felt better. From an emotional standpoint, I was not at full capacity. Though I had tried to let go of the past, I found that some wounds stay pink forever. I would never get over Pinky, and I was okay with that. My wife and I had come to a peace as well. After our initial separation, I was immediately alienated from her, followed by years and years of bitter exchanges, something that only fueled our resentment toward one another. What I couldn't understand at the time was that my wife also needed to heal. Again, it was a case of my being selfish. I was home now. I had been wronged in my career. My oldest son had taken his life. *Who was going to help me?* My wife had suffered just as much. Maybe even more. *Where was I when she needed me?* We would both dig in for years, trying to pick up the pieces of our lives. Eventually, I would discover that resentment dies a lot like love does. It becomes too much work. It's so much easier to just let things go. Ultimately, we both realized it was a better way to raise the grandchildren Pinky left behind. And we did just that.

    My transition from "no father" to "grandfather" and then back to "father" was instrumental in my own growth and healing. My faith in God had not completely returned, but I found it interesting that all it took for me to start healing was to help heal others. That is what I tried to do with my grandchildren. Remarkably, my own kids had done quite well in my absence. My daughter Crystal had managed to turn out amazing in every way. She was an outstanding student who was her class valedictorian. She graduated cum laude from California Baptist University and even got her doctorate at USC. My other daughter Tiffany was equally accomplished and grounded. I couldn't be prouder of my boys as well. While I loved them all dearly and am still their biggest fan, I have to credit my wife for the bulk of their success. But the lion's share of parenting "Little Hector," who as a boy had watched his father blow his own head off, would largely fall on me.

I can't honestly say what it's like to be a father, because I was never a good one. But my son Pinky was a *great father*. Until he had slipped into his horrible state of depression, he took his kids everywhere. He went to every little league game they played in. He drove them to school every day. He picked them up every day. Even on the days when his car was in service, he would still take them to school, throwing them on the back of his bicycle. I never saw Pinky without his kids. Needless to say, his death — and the manner in which he died — was an unspeakable blow to Little Hector.

Little Hector moved in with me after his father died. I had plenty of room on my ranch. It was beautiful. And it was a place that went a long way in fostering an atmosphere of tranquility in my life. But Little Hector didn't take to it like I had hoped. There is a natural disconnect between all fathers and sons that is generational. Every generation of kids grows up in a different culture with different pressures. Yes, you can say they are all relative, but it's hard to understand what you really *don't understand*. I never had to deal with gangs, cell phones or social media. I didn't know what it was like to do my school work on a computer or what to do if someone sent me an inappropriate attachment on my email. I also came from a generation that inherently did not seek counseling. I was raised, as were most of my friends, with the principle that if I had a problem, I had to deal with it and try not to make it someone else's. The fact that we were Spanish-Mexican Americans, arguably the most macho culture on the planet, didn't make matters easier. We didn't ask for help. *Even when we needed it.*

Little Hector did need help. He was truant. He had joined a gang. He started doing drugs. I didn't know what the hell to do. But for him, I would do what I would never do for myself: I asked for help. The first place I went was to his school to speak to his counselors. They had not even been informed that Little Hector had lost his father. When they heard how, they were ashamed. They rallied to help turn his life around. Little Hector received the counseling he desperately needed and as a physical outlet, I enrolled him into one of the best boxing academies in Riverside. I can't tell you what a joy it was to watch Little Hector take root and grow. He was an animal at the boxing gym. Though not the most gifted of fighters, pound for pound, he was certainly one of the gym's toughest.

At the end of the day, I can honestly say that Little Hector and his brother are the reason I am alive today. While I am so grateful to my wife for standing by me, and for my own sons' and daughters' unconditional love, it was Pinky's boys who really gave my life a purpose. In a strange way, I think my son Pinky's suicide actually saved my life. Had I not had his boys to take care of, I would've been engulfed in the flames of my own bitterness. I was forced to carry on by something that was bigger than me: *Mi familia.*

After I received the call, I shared it with my mother who wept. As she did, I thought about what the caller had told me. *Time to stop hiding and start living.* I was going to do both. First I was going to do something else: I was going to start talking.

To everyone.

· · · · ·

The Last Narc

Not even two months after I had received the wonderful news that Mexico could no longer enforce its extradition against me, I was able to secure an interview with Fox News host Megyn Kelly. Interestingly, only weeks before my own emancipation, someone else associated with my past had also gone free. He also happened to be, in all likelihood, the chief conspirator in the abduction, torture and murder of Kiki Camarena. It was Rafael Caro Quintero, who had been held in a Mexican prison for over 20 years. Mexico ignored a U.S. extradition request and never informed Washington of his release. Two days later, the White House released a statement saying it was "deeply concerned" Quintero was free. Fox News had reached out to me to offer my analysis on Quintero's role in the Camarena case and I was happy to do so.

The interview went splendidly as I gave my unique insight into the case that had so consumed me for decades.

"Camarena was kidnapped and murdered because he came up with the idea that we needed to chase the money, not the drugs," I said. "We were seizing a huge amount of drugs. But we were not really disrupting the cartels."

I couldn't believe how thrilled I was to be talking about it. It was like the chained muzzle around my neck and mouth had snapped and I was finally free to speak. The interview segued into the role the DFS had played in the tragic case. I minced no words.

"Back in the mid-1980s, the DFS's main role was to protect the drug lords. Drug smugglers/transporters employed by Quintero were always provided protection prior to moving a drug load. DFS agents accompanied the smugglers at all times to avoid any problems."

Megyn seemed fascinated by the charge and allowed me to go on. So I did.

"After the murder of Camarena, Mexico's investigation pointed out that the DFS had been complicit along with American intelligence in the kidnapping and torture of Kiki. That's when they decided to disband the DFS."

I could hear the deafening silence at this statement. Ms. Kelly asked me to clarify how I knew for certain U.S. officials were "complicit." I made it as clear as I could.

"The CIA was the source. They were there."

Then I spoke about what I had discovered from my informants from the Mexican state police, who were also there and witnessed Kiki's interrogation and positively identified photos of CIA operatives.

I said all of this, not in a sensationalistic manner or tone, but as a simple matter-of-fact.

· · · · ·

As soon as the interview was aired, my phone started blowing up. I received calls from friends, former agents, family. I had hoped to hear, "Wow, Hector, you looked great! What an interesting interview!" Instead, I heard dozens of varied expressions that all tried to convey the same message: *"Hector, are you out of your fucking mind?"*

I didn't know that I had stepped on a hornet's nest. I was just so happy to be free to talk about the case that defined my career. Obviously, I understood that it was still an open investigation, but I wasn't presenting any new information to the masses. My witnesses had all testified in public and transcripts of their pre-trial and trial testimony were easily accessible. Further, given the time that had passed since Kiki's death and the fact that there were still so many unanswered questions, I thought it was responsible to at least begin a dialogue of the event. *After all, didn't we want to get to the truth? Isn't that what justice is supposed to be about?* I guess not.

While I didn't receive any offers to speak with other news networks, dozens of writers reached out and wanted to hear more about my story. One was an author I was quite familiar with named Charles Bowden. "Chuck" as I came to call him was a brilliant writer who wrote some amazing books that covered the same ground I was all too familiar with. In 2006, he wrote the groundbreaking *Kill the Messenger: How the CIA's Crack-Cocaine Controversy Destroyed Journalist Gary Webb*. Years later, he also wrote *El Sicario: The Autobiography of a Mexican Assassin* with his partner and editor Molly Molloy. Chuck had seen the interview on Fox News and when we talked, he explained just how deep the rabbit hole of drugs, the CIA and the Mexican cartels went. Chuck believed every word of my story, but being the professional he was, asked if he could interview my witnesses. I let him speak with them and he was so moved by their conviction to the truth he decided he wanted to write my story. I was over the moon. Chuck had intended to write a book, but as a means to acquire a book deal, he pitched the idea for a three part novella on the website *Matter*. Again, he would collaborate with Molly Molloy, and the result would be the brilliant piece of work *Blood on the Corn*.

Though I didn't know Chuck for long, the two of us became incredibly close while working together. Writing is not just a collaborative endeavor, it is both self-revealing and intimate. I had to share aspects of my life and work with Chuck that I had never shared with anyone. He was never judging. Always honest. Always encouraging me to dig deeper into myself. I came to love Chuck Bowden, and I was heartbroken, in a very different way, when news came to me that he had suddenly died just months before the piece was scheduled to run. I wasn't heartbroken because I had lost the writer for my book. I was heartbroken because I had lost a friend. I hadn't had one in some time. And it felt good.

After Chuck Bowden and Molly Malloy's superb novella was released in November 2014, a few other writers followed suit. Jason McGahan wrote an excellent piece for *L.A. Weekly* the following summer. The highly respected Mexican writer J. Jesús Esquivel, who had written blistering pieces on the narco-politics of Mexico for over a decade in one of the country's most prestigious periodicals, *Proceso*, wrote a Spanish language book entitled *La CIA, Camarena, and Caro Quintero: La historia secreta*, published in February 2015. While all three of the works were excellent in their execution, storytelling and research, none seemed to push the Kiki Camarena case into the public conversation. Another medium would send Kiki, the Guadalajara Cartel and the entire drug world from Mexico through South America into the pop-culture stratosphere. It was a little TV show that premiered in the summer of 2015 on a streaming network I had never heard of.

It was called *Narcos*.

Chapter 28

Miedo a la verdad
Fear of the Truth

Despite having worked and lived in Los Angeles for many years, I am not an "Angeleno." I liked the Dodgers, but never got into the Lakers. I could care less about Hollywood and its glitz and glamour. Don't get me wrong, I enjoyed a good movie now and then, but I never felt any affinity to show business just because I spent a lot of time in L.A. So I was far from excited when I received a call from someone at *Narcos* who said the show's creator would like to talk to me. By this time in early 2016, I had heard of the show but had never seen it. I knew it had something to do with the DEA hunting and bringing down Pablo Escobar, but was told it took great artistic license and was more fictional than what actually occurred. I had no interest in seeing it one way or another. I had lived that life. Why would I want to be entertained by it? I was told that the show was immensely popular and that producers were looking to hire "consultants" for their new storylines. I said, "Okay. Sounds good to me." I asked if the job paid well and they told me how much I would make. Then I thought to myself, *okay, sounds even better.*

I ended up meeting with *Narcos'* creator Eric Newman and a couple of the writers on the staff. It was my first "Hollywood" meeting and I have to say, I was pretty excited because I didn't know what to expect. My excitement waned quickly as the process of scheduling the meeting dragged on and on. There was a series of phone calls and emails with directions and passes and instructions. It would be scheduled then "pushed" then re-scheduled. *What the fuck?* I had met the president of the United States once and all it took was for one of his Secret Service members to tap me on the shoulder. My meeting with *Narcos* took more planning than I did for the raid at Limoncito.

Pain in the ass notwithstanding, everything about the meeting was terrific. Netflix, the network that streamed *Narcos,* treated me first class all the way. Everyone from security to the assistants were polite, respectful and accommodating. The office itself was electric with activity, sharply-dressed folks talking on their Bluetooths, listening to pitches, speaking with clients. I had a great feeling being there — and this feeling was magnified by my confidence that I could really offer the show and its writers some incredible storylines. Aside from the actual stories, I could offer insight into how things *really happened.* I'm not an idiot. I knew the show wasn't a documentary, but I had given it a brief look before my meeting and my first thought was, *why not make it more real?* I knew there was a way to incorporate some of my ideas without sacrificing their storytelling.

I didn't think my meeting itself could have gone any better. The writers in the room were rapt with attention as I shared some of my adventures in Mazatlán. I told them about my shootout at Limoncito. I told them about the drug dealer who had been thrown from the plane. Then I began to tell them about the Camarena murder. And I told them *everything.*

Eric Newman had been silent, listening for much of the meeting as I rambled on. While the writers waited on every word that spilled out of my mouth, he just stared at me, interested but poker-faced. I told them about the DFS' involvement. I told them about Felix Rodriguez and the CIA. I also told them about a certain DEA agent who was known to be dirty and may have also been complicit in Kiki's death.

They. Could. Not. Believe. It.

When the meeting was done, I felt great. I shook everyone's hands. They thanked me profusely and made it *very clear* that they would be reaching out to me very soon.

They didn't.

• • • • •

After my interview with the *Narcos* team, I was on a high. The idea of sharing some of my stories as well as my explosive insight into the murder of Kiki Camarena had me thrilled. In addition to the *Narcos* opportunity, I had been introduced to a very gifted and accomplished documentarian named Tiller Russell who was also interested in my story. He wanted to do it as a limited docuseries for Amazon. It seemed as if finally, after over two decades of being gagged, I was going to get to tell the truth to the world one way or another.

It was splitting hairs as to who I wanted to go with. On the one hand, everyone was telling me that the potential Netflix opportunity was far greater. It seemed as if overnight the general public had become obsessed with the world of drug cartels. *Narcos* was now a global phenomenon and becoming a household name.

But there was something about telling the story in its truest form, documentary, that had me equally as excited. Unlike a scripted version of events, I could get to tell my own story — the way it really happened. I never got to make the choice whether to go with Netflix or Amazon. That choice was made for me.

As days turned to weeks, Netflix and *Narcos* seemed to sour on me. While they had made a tacit offer, it was much lower than they originally had told me, and they also seemed generally uninterested in my version of events during the Camarena case. I could tell something was up. I'm not the type of person who lets things fester without an answer, so I called up Eric Newman and asked him point blank, "Eric, what's going on?"

Eric hesitated a moment, then hemmed and hawed before he said, "You know, Hector. Apparently, you're a very polarizing character within the DEA."

"Of course I am," I said. "I tell the truth."

Newman dug in. "No. People don't like you."

"People like who?"

"People you used to work with."

Ahhh... I thought to myself. *He's been talking to that dirty DEA agent.....* My blood began to boil and I said, "You mean the agent who testified for Rubén Zuno Arce when he was being tried for murdering Kiki? The same guy who my witnesses say they saw take money from their cartel bosses?"

I took a moment to calm down then said in my most serious tone, "This is something that I would like you to pass along to *that agent*. It's not that he doesn't like me. *He fears me.*"

Our conversation ended shortly after that and I never heard from him again.

It didn't matter. As soon as I got off the phone, I reached out to Tiller Russell and we talked about the documentary.

·····

Regarding my dalliance with Netflix and *Narcos*, I am absolutely grateful that I did not end up going down that road creatively. Though the call was not mine to make, there was no way in hell that I would have allowed them to tell the version of events that took place in *Narcos: Mexico*, which centered around Kiki's abduction, torture and murder. When it came out, I was deeply troubled by it. I understand the nature of entertainment. I know "based on true events" doesn't really mean much at all. But as I tried to sit through it, it became so glaringly apparent that the shows' creators, writers, directors and producers were being absolutely irresponsible with historical events that should have been treated as sacrosanct. By fictionalizing Kiki's story, they were doing a disservice to his true legacy — as well as the legacy of all the agents who worked their hearts out to help solve his case. It did the opposite to the Guadalajara Cartel and their leaders. First of all, it glamorized that life. Yes, I get it. "Wish fulfillment" is why people want to watch. But the show goes further to try to "humanize" people that were sub-human. An example that made me sick to my stomach was when Kiki, in the middle of his torture, is given a break to have dinner with Gallardo. What. The. Fuck. If the show's creators and writers were going to such great lengths to create one of the most absurd scenes imaginable in the spirit of "poetic license," *why even use real names? What was the point?*

The most egregious sin Netflix and *Narcos: Mexico* committed was that their story gave a pass to many of those responsible for the crimes against Kiki. This is not because of ignorance. I sat in Eric Newman's office and told them what actually happened. But I suppose the truth isn't as good for business as perpetuating the lies and myths that have been associated with Camarena's death since February of 1985. In this sense, and I have said it publicly, Netflix and *Narcos: Mexico* are complicit in covering up the actual facts of Kiki Camarena's abduction, torture and murder. *And for that?* Shame on them.

Chapter 29

Vaquero
Cowboy

It's the spring of 2019, but it's hot as summer in the San Gabriel Valley where I am riding my favorite horse, Jasper. After Pinky's death — and my near brush with it — I finally put aside my feelings of loss, guilt and depression to help raise his grandchildren. Once his children grew, healed and became grounded, many of my feelings of despair returned. In order to combat those negative emotions, I began raising horses. I've always loved being around horses, so I purchased and raised colt Andalusians and Friesians. As soon as they came of age, which is around two years old, I would start riding and training them. One thing led to another and before I knew it, I owned 12 of those beautiful animals. I hired a professional trainer, Alejandro Luna, who had attended a horse training school in Spain, and he and I started working together.

    I know that animals can have a very calming effect on people. But there is something about horses that is transcending. Maybe it's because for centuries we humans have shared such a unique bond with them. I compared the human relationship with horses to that of canines in an earlier chapter and I think that's accurate. If they like you, they follow you around like puppies. They are affectionate, loyal and unconditional in their love. In all honesty, the love of a horse is far richer. They're not just big stuffed animals you feed and pet. *They carry your weight. They work for you.* And at times, they seem to know you better than you even know yourself. But I would say my relationship with horses goes even deeper. My deep connection with them also helped me to reconnect with the roots of my own family, and in turn, *with myself.* My ancestors were adventurers. Protectors. Cowboys. They endured pain, betrayal and heartbreak long before I ever was. They were the ones who shed light upon my darkness. They were the ones who carried me when I had fallen and didn't have the strength to pull myself up. My hope is that, in some way, my struggles and my triumphs and my suffering can help the future generations of my family. My prayer is that when they are in need, they will also come to realize that there is no resurrection without a crucifixion.

It seems like my whole life has brought me back to the beginning. Maybe that's really why I became a cop, a DEA agent and investigator. I wanted to find out how everything started. How it began. From tree resin to ash. From fury to light. From wonder to awareness.

My mother was a woman who could see the future. I am no longer a man who is haunted by the past. Though the past will always be "a part" of me, it will also be *apart from me.* It does not define me. Nor does it direct me. For much of my adult life I have lived with a thorn in my heart. I have lived with shame and shadow. But when I think of my father and my son, I am reminded that *la luz desplaza la sombra.* The light displaces the shadow. Though it has been largely the love of my God, my family and my friends, ultimately, it is ourselves who must radiate the light to dispel the dark. So this is what I try to do. Every day of my life.

The Last Narc

· · · · ·

Jasper was in a good mood that day. He was listening well. Riding strong. Sharp. Strange how even animals have moods. I wonder if he ever thinks to himself, *Gee, Hector is in a lousy mood today.* If Jasper could sense my mood (and I think he can), he might have been thinking, *Hector is on point today. He's sharp. Happy.* Because the two of us are. We're both happy. We both know we're practicing for a scene in my Amazon documentary.

Our director, Tiller Russell, has told us the footage may not make the final cut, but we both want to be ready for it. We both want to look good for the documentary's big finale which features me with my shirt off, riding a dancing Jasper. Like cowboy boots, hats and belt buckles, having the best horse is also big with Mexican cowboys. And in the end, that's who I am. A cowboy.

· · · · ·

My name is Hector and I am a Berrellez. I am not the first one in my family to know betrayal. That treachery had already been etched into my DNA. So too was the grace that I discovered by enduring, believing and accepting that all the things in my life happen for a reason.

Just as they did my ancestors.

It has taken me a lifetime to understand how the past and present are chained together. For my story, it is a chain that includes the magic of adventure, the sum of sacrifice, the pain of loss and betrayal, and the poetry of faith.

And it was all forged long before I existed.

Epilogue

By the end of my career with the DEA, I had concluded that the rise in illegal drug use in the United States in the 1980s, especially the crack cocaine epidemic, was the result of the CIA inundating the streets of our inner cities with pure cocaine — all to support a secret and unlawful war in Nicaragua. It did not matter that we were creating a generation of drug-addicted zombies here in America, nor that we were fueling violent street gangs in our cities (the Bloods and Crips, for example) who constantly fought over drug-selling turf, resulting in thousands of deaths. Not to mention the thousands of Americans that died yearly of drug overdoses and the hundreds of thousands of Americans we imprisoned for using and selling illegal drugs. Our country made huge profits from these poor miserable souls.

As a special agent with the DEA, I was assigned to foreign posts and frequently travelled throughout Central and South America conducting drug investigations. I saw with my own eyes how powerful drug lords are. They have the ability to install their chosen people in government, and they also have the power to topple governments that oppose them. In Mexico, for instance, government officials installed by the drug lords ensure that these drug lords receive law enforcement and military protection.

The CIA is strictly an intelligence agency with no law enforcement authority, designed to deal with issues and problems outside of the United States. They are the world's premiere spy agency running covert operations throughout the world. They operate outside constitutional authority and take whatever action is necessary to protect the national security of the United States. I know, I conducted black operations with them, operations that I can never reveal. The CIA, under the color of protecting the national security of the United States, has historically aligned itself with criminal elements. In the 1980s, the CIA needed assistance in funding a secret war in Nicaragua, a war that was not authorized by Congress and the American people. To fund it, the CIA aligned itself with Colombian and Mexican drug cartels. In Colombia they partnered with Pablo Escobar, leader of the Medellín Cartel, and in Mexico they partnered with the Guadalajara Cartel. Both cartels contributed billions of dollars to the Nicaraguan Contra freedom fighters, a fact supported by Ramon Milan's congressional testimony before the Kerry Commission. When I complained about this nefarious partnership to a high level CIA official, he said to me, "Listen Hector, the Russians and Cubans are providing full military and financial assistance to the communist regime of Daniel Ortega in Nicaragua. The Russians and Cubans do not adhere to constitutional authority and neither can we if we are to compete against them on a level playing field. So we are compelled to operate outside of constitutional authority and do whatever it takes to preserve our national security."

When even huge drug seizures had no negative impact on the availability of drugs in the United States, Kiki Camarena suggested implementing investigative measures to go after the cartel's drug profits. In the years between 1982 and 1989, the Guadalajara Cartel was making $5 billion a year in drug profits. Ernesto Fonseca Carrillo, who kept large amounts of monies in the basements of numerous homes he owned, complained of losing over $3 million a month to rats. Miguel Ángel Félix Gallardo was running $20 million a month through a Bank of America account in San Diego. The banks did not care that they were receiving narco dollars. The CIA did not care either, because Gallardo was contributing millions of Guadalajara Cartel narco dollars to the CIA to support their "secret war" in Nicaragua. The Contra war took precedence over law enforcement operations, and the CIA withheld evidence of Contra crimes and corruption, all in the name of national security.

The U.S. press is also to blame for the drug corruption problem that existed in the 1980s and 1990s. Even as a tsunami of drugs and drug profits was flooding across our border from Mexico, the United States government, echoed by the press, praised the Mexican kleptocracy run by the corrupt Salinas family as "reform-minded" and championed closer ties between the United States and Mexico. The fact that the DEA was reporting and providing evidence that the president's brother Raul Salinas was landing 747 passengers planes, each loaded with 20 tons of cocaine in plain daylight at the Mexico City International Airport, fell on deaf ears.

When investigative reporter Gary Webb of the *San Jose Mercury News* wrote his first articles in 1996 linking the CIA, the drug traffickers and the Nicaraguan contras, the *Washington Post* and *Los Angeles Times* went out of their way to discredit Webb's groundbreaking reporting. *Was it simply due to jealousy, stupidity, and incompetence? Or was it because of pressure, intimidation or influence by the CIA?* How could it be that two major newspaper outlets rushed to assist the CIA in concealing their alliances with and protection of some of the world's major drug lords? This makes me suspect that these and other news agencies are on the payroll of the CIA. I know for a fact that the CIA pays foreign reporters to spin stories in their favor. *Why could it not happen here in the United States?*

Even with most of its leadership in prison or dead, remnants of the mighty Guadalajara Cartel have survived into the 21st century. But because they lack the unity and collective power of the cartel that spawned them, they may be even more dangerous. These new cartels have terrorized the whole nation, instilling fear throughout a populace governed by a useless, ineffective, inept and corrupt government. Their methods of terror include decapitations, dismemberments, castrations and public hangings of any persons considered an enemy of their lucrative and illegal businesses. These new cartels — the Sinaloa, Juarez, Gulf, Los Zetas, Beltran Leyvas, La Familia Michoacana, Nueva Generacion and others — do not adhere to the strict standing rule of the old Guadalajara Cartel: "No intervention with the good citizens of Mexico." Instead, they patrol the streets accompanied by corrupt police and military officials, extorting monies from hard working businessmen, abducting and raping young girls and killing anyone that complains or dares to oppose them. In September 2014, corrupt cops working for the cartels captured 43 college students near the town of Iguala in the state of Guerrero. These young men and women were tortured, mutilated and murdered, and after six years none of their bodies have been found and positively identified. A team of foreign forensic investigators found evidence of involvement by the Mexican Army and the federal police in the disappearance of these students, but they had to leave Mexico when the government refused to accept this incriminating evidence. In June 2014, in the town of Tlatlaya in Estado de Mexico, 22 young people were made to stand up against a wall before being shot to death by Mexican soldiers.

The carnage continues. As recent as November 5th, 2019, nine members of the LeBaron Mormon family were slaughtered on a highway near La Mora, Sonora, Mexico. Thirteen LeBaron family members (all women and children) had been traveling from the United States to Mexico to attend a wedding when they were intercepted by Sinaloa Cartel gunmen who opened fire on them with automatic weapons. Some of the children escaped by fleeing into the desert, but three babies strapped in baby chairs who escaped the fusillade were burnt to death by these vicious animals. President Donald Trump, who was very upset about this heinous attack on innocent Americans, complained to Mexico's President Andres Lopez Obrador, suggested going to war against these out of control cartels and offered to dispatch Navy Seals, Marines and Army Special Forces to Mexico to once and for all obliterate them. President Obrador's answer was that a war was what he was trying to prevent, and that he was going to fight the drug war with *"abrazos, no balazos,"* with hugs, not bullets. Obrador's absurd philosophy, and the fact that he appointed Manuel Bartlett Diáz (who was linked to the murders of journalist Manuel Buendía Tellezgirón, and Kiki Camarena) to his cabinet makes me question his integrity, honesty and trustworthiness. To date, no arrests have been made for the murders of the LeBaron family.

During El Chapo's trial in New York, witnesses implicated officials at every level of the Mexican government in taking bribes. Numerous witnesses testified that El Chapo paid former Mexican President Enrique Peña Nieto $100 million to come out of hiding after his first escape from a Mexican prison. According to witnesses, President Obrador's former top security official Genaro García Luna received multi-millions in bribe monies to protect El Chapo and the operations of the Sinaloa Cartel. García was arrested in the United States this year, and is currently in custody facing charges of taking bribes and money laundering. The Sinaloa Cartel is so powerful that when Mexican army soldiers recently detained one of El Chapo's sons and were holding him in the military garrison in Culiacán, Sinaloa, over 400 gunmen surrounded the military garrison and ordered him released, threatening to kill all military members stationed there. The defendant was immediately released and the central government has done nothing to bring those involved to justice. This incident is just one example of how corrupt and inept the government of Mexico has become. Mexico is a failed state that can no longer protect its citizens. Other societies should study Colombia and Mexico to learn the corrosive effects of government corruption.

In Mexico, the cartel leaders are corrupt government officials who operate behind the scenes. Presently, the Sinaloa Cartel is operating under the direction and protection of cabinet level government officials including Manuel Bartlett Diáz. The Nueva Generación (New Generation) Cartel, the second largest in Mexico, is receiving protection from the governor of the state of Jalisco, Enrique Alfaro, a member of the ousted PRI party. The PRI party, wanting to retain its power, provides guidance and protection to Nueva Generación.

The Sinaloa and Nueva Generación Cartels are constantly at war with each other, as they serve opposing political parties. The poor citizens of Mexico are caught in the middle. Thousands are murdered monthly for opposing the cartels, refusing to pay extortion monies — even going as far as surrendering their own children to them.

The solution to destroying the cartels would not be very difficult. First, cut off their heads. That means kill their leaders. Period. Second, expose and arrest the top government officials who protect the cartel drug lords. Third, eviscerate their crops. Done. We could end the War on Drugs in less than a week. Unfortunately, we will do none of the above. The truth is, and I have been saying it for years: *They don't want it to end.*

But there is hope.

As you have read, I have dedicated almost my entire life to the battle against illegal narcotics. For me, the battle was always very personal because of my younger brother's heroin addiction when I was coming of age. But as my fight took me from small-town cop all the way to the head of one of the largest investigations in the history of the DEA, I learned something that it took me a long time to fully comprehend. *I am not alone.* The War on Drugs has deeply affected every citizen on both sides of the border. I am reminded of something I heard from a woman I met long ago, back when I was working in Mexico. Her son had been a low-level member of the cartel and had been found dead in Jalisco. I happened to be there when his mother came to identify the body. Naturally, it was not my first encounter with a mother who mourned the loss of her son. There was so much death all the time that I had become that indifferent authority who stood by soberly in the face of tragedy. As I watched the woman study the bloodied body of her son, I was struck by her stoicism. No wailing. No sobbing. She just stared at the boy. As she did, I thought about the vicious cycle of death that drugs cause, and that at its very core, it's always a grieving family at the very center that suffers. After a long, uncomfortable silence, I muttered the standard, "I'm sorry."

Without taking her gaze off the boy, she asked me, *"Tiene hijos, señor?"*

Do you have children, sir?

I nodded.

"¿Los amas?" she asked.

Do you love them?

"Sí," I said.

"Algún día, cuando todos amemos a nuestros hijos más que nada, todo esto terminará," she said.

Someday, when we all love our children more than anything, this will all end.

Then she walked away.

It was the best and most articulate take on the War on Drugs I would ever hear.

Publisher's Note

The Author and Renaissance Literary & Talent have attempted to create this book with the highest quality conversion. However, should you notice any errors within this text please e-mail corrections@renaissancemgmt.net with the title/author in the subject line and the corrections in the body of the e-mail. Thank you for your help and patronage.

Printed in Great Britain
by Amazon